THE
TIMES SQUARE
HUSTLER

THE
TIMES SQUARE
HUSTLER

Male Prostitution in New York City

Robert P. McNamara

Westport, Connecticut
London

Library of Congress Cataloging-in-Publication Data

McNamara, Robert P.
    The Times Square hustler : male prostitution in New York City /
Robert P. McNamara.
        p.   cm.
    Includes bibliographical references and index.
    ISBN 0–275–95003–4 (alk. paper)—ISBN 0–275–95186–3 (pbk.)
    1. Male prostitution—New York (N.Y.).   2. Male prostitutes—New
York (N.Y.).   I. Title.
    HQ146.N7M24   1994
    306.74′3′097471—dc20   94–21689

British Library Cataloguing in Publication Data is available.

Library of Congress Catalog Card Number: 94–21689
ISBN: 0–275–95003–4
        0–275–95186–3 (pbk.)

First published in 1994

Praeger Publishers, 88 Post Road West, Westport, CT 06881
An imprint of Greenwood Publishing Group, Inc.

Printed in the United States of America

The paper used in this book complies with the
Permanent Paper Standard issued by the National
Information Standards Organization (Z39.48–1984).

10 9 8 7 6 5 4

To Dan and Maryann: The risks were many and the chances of success small, but you helped anyway. I owe you my life and love you both for giving it back to me. Thank you for gambling on such a long shot.

And to Kristy: You have taught me the meaning of trust, compassion, and to see the good in people. Although I may not always be the best student, there are few who try harder and no one who loves you more.

Contents

Illustrations

MAP

TABLES

Preface

My interest in this subject began with an interest in AIDS and its impact on high-risk groups. I sought to find groups of people at high risk of infection in order to learn something about how they cope with the risks associated with AIDS. Since male prostitutes frequently engage in the three primary means of transmission of the virus—unprotected sex with males, unprotected sex with females, and intravenous (IV) drug use and needle sharing—they are a group at high risk of infection with the human immunodeficiency virus (HIV). This is especially true in New York City where AIDS is widespread and where, particularly in Times Square, the sex trade has a long history.

I went into this area looking for people at high risk of infection, but once there, I realized that there is a sense of community among this population. I was drawn to the folkways of the hustling community in Times Square and as a result, the project became more of a community study. After only a short time I realized that this community was on the verge of change.

There were three major pressures affecting the shape of the community and the characteristics of life within it. First, AIDS is a prevalent theme among young hustlers. They are at exceptionally high risk and the methods they use to cope with the disease are an important part of the "life." Second, the influence of crack cocaine has changed the relationship between hustler and client as well as the relationships among the boys themselves. Finally, gentrification of the Times Square area has resulted in a major shift in the nature and location of the trade. It has also altered the boys' perceptions of hustling and their place in it. These three events have had such an impact on hustling in Times Square that they are changing the very character of the trade, and, at the same time, changing the shape of the community.

I have been extremely fortunate to have had a multitude of people help me in this project. My wife, Kristy, deserves special consideration since she read and reread chapters and helped me clarify my thoughts as well as my prose. She also deserves credit for enduring the many conversations I have had with people about the study.

I also owe a great debt of thanks to Albert J. Reiss, Jr., Kai Erikson, and Nancy Swanson. Much of my understanding of field research can be attributed to Albert Reiss, who taught me to look beyond the immediately observable to the unobserved because therein often lies the truly significant. Another important piece of wisdom he imparted to me was the way in which one extracts the sociological significance of field research. During the project, he made sure my sociological cap remained fixed in place. These are the two most important lessons he could have given me, and I will always be grateful for them.

A true craftsman of prose, Kai's insightful thoughts and sensitive observations helped me capture and tell the story of hustling. He taught me more about "telling a tale" than he realizes. Additionally, Nancy Swanson has been a indefatigable source of support and has helped immeasurably in organizing and conceptualizing the findings of the project.

Bill Kornblum and Terry Williams also merit thanks. Most of what I know about the Times Square scene came from my many conversations with them. They also introduced me to numerous people who helped along the way. Additionally, their gracious hospitality while I was in New York will never be forgotten. I have benefited greatly from knowing them and will always be in their debt.

I would also like to thank several others who provided me with valuable information and insight. They are truly exceptional individuals who do not conform to perceptions about the "typical" New Yorker. They include Deputy Inspector Ed Forker of the Port Authority Police, Shane Newmark of the Urban Development Corporation, Art Milks of the Metropolitan Transit Authority, and Bill Daly from the Mayor's Office of Midtown Enforcement. Special thanks also goes to J. Dan Cover of Furman University, Susan Henry of the APT Foundation, Eugene Fappiano of Southern Connecticut State University, and Officer Walt Faust of the Waterbury Connecticut Police Department for their help and support.

I am also indebted to Leslie Hartmann for her critical eye and editorial skills, while Ann Fitzpatrick and Pam Colesworthy merit thanks for their help in my interactions with the Yale University bureaucracy. In a similar way, I would like to thank Jim Ice, Marsha Goldstein, Bridget Austiguy, Liz Murphy, and the staff at Greenwood Publishing Group for their assistance in this project. Producing a book is often a difficult task, but the staff at Praeger has made this process a relatively painless one. I should also extend my thanks to all the hustlers of Times Square and especially my three key informants: Apache, Raul, and Flacco. Their help was crucial to the success of this project.

Finally, I would like to extend my heartfelt thanks to Dennis Kenney, who helped me find the path of academia and has always been supportive and encouraging in my professional pursuits. I owe him more than he can ever realize. Thank you, Dennis, for your wisdom, advice, and help, and above all, for believing in me.

THE
TIMES SQUARE
HUSTLER

1

Hustling and the Marketplace

Historically, male prostitution has taken many forms, including "escort boys," those who worked in brothels, and even "kept boys," who served more as a companion to a client than a prostitute (Coombs 1974; Drew and Drake 1969; Weisberg 1985). While research on the subject of male prostitutes is still relatively sparse, there have been a few attempts to examine this population. For instance, the now classic study by Reiss (1961) found that most of the boys view prostitution as a job or simply a means of making money. He also found a normative system operating to limit the scope of activities in which the boys could or would engage.

Other studies have attempted to identify common characteristics and describe the various motivations for becoming involved in prostitution (Weisberg 1985; Butts 1947; Jersild 1956; Ross 1959; Luckenbill 1986a, 1986b, 1985; Lloyd 1983; Campagna and Poffenberger 1988; James 1982; MacNamara 1965; West 1991; Bracey 1989). Most of the recent research has focused on the risks of AIDS and on the runaway population.

For instance, Lauderback and Waldorf (1989) interviewed 180 male street prostitutes and 180 escort boys in San Francisco and found that almost two-thirds had been tested for HIV. Ten percent of the street hustlers and almost 25% of the escort boys were HIV positive. Additionally, most of the boys had a high level of understanding about AIDS and HIV, and condom use for anal intercourse was frequent. About half these boys were IV drug users and most had known someone with HIV or AIDS, which could explain the relatively high percentage who understood the disease (see also Ross, 1988; Elifson, Boles, and Sweat 1993; Calhoun and Pickerill 1988; Morse et al. 1991; Pleak and Meyer-Bahlburg 1990; Borus-Rotheram and Koopman 1991).

Thus, while it appears there is a growing body of AIDS related literature on this population, little is known about hustling in Times Square and even less is known about the ways in which hustlers develop a sense of cohesion as they share similar experiences. Part of the explanation is found in the way in which prostitution is practiced. In Times Square, male prostitution is more of an entrepreneurial activity occurring in an organized market area than is generally the case elsewhere. It is referred to colloquially as "hustling," a term whose meanings can include the activities of confidence men, drug dealers, those who deal with stolen merchandise and, in general, individuals who engage in a variety of illegal activities. However, the label "hustler" is also applied to males who engage in various sexual activities with other males for money, illegal drugs, or some other form of payment.

Hustling is incorporated into the definition of prostitution since the person seeks out and attempts to entice as many clients as possible without the benefit of a broker, client list, or other type of intermediary. Thus, hustling in Times Square is less organized than other forms of prostitution and is more like a type of localized market activity.

THE MARKETPLACE

Times Square possesses certain characteristics and institutions that facilitate prostitution. For instance, the peep shows, porno shops, hotels, bars, and the Port Authority Bus Terminal not only offer a centralized locale for the sex market, they also provide places for hustlers and clients to meet and carry out their transactions. Additionally, the influx of people who use the terminal and peep shows produces a steady supply of patrons to the market.

Virtually all these organizations are profit making, and the economic benefits they derive from hustling foster the acceptance of prostitution. This is especially true of the hotels and peep shows, which have strong economic links to the sex trade. Consequently, the nature of hustling is predicated on the existence of these types of organizations as well as the manner in which they allow this type of activity to occur.

Moreover, the Port Authority Bus Terminal provides the market with a diurnal quality. In many ways, hustling is dependent on the work schedule of commuters and its frequency coincides with rush hours;

hustlers are very busy early in the morning, as people make their way to work, and in the early evening, as they return home. There are also a number of older men who reside in the Times Square area who are either retired or living on public assistance. They, too, regularly solicit hustlers and know that the terminal serves as a central meeting place.

Another feature of the hustling market involves the activity's occupational structure. Because the vast majority of hustlers have few, if any, other means of economic support, hustling in Times Square is viewed as an income-producing activity. For most, it is a full-time job. While some are receiving public assistance, which would normally reduce participation in the trade, these hustlers usually have wives and children to support. Thus, the need to earn a living from hustling remains important.

In this way, hustling can be seen as an occupation for almost all the participants. Another illustration of this occupational role is demonstrated by the fact that most of the hustlers do not reside in the market area. In fact, many live outside Manhattan and, like so many other workers, must commute to Times Square every day. Additionally, part of the market is organized for the hustlers themselves. For instance, there are certain bars or parks where hustlers meet to socialize only with friends and colleagues. As I describe in subsequent pages, these places hold particular importance for hustlers.

In sum, there is a local market in which hustling exists, and it has a certain organization. There is a sense of territoriality in that it is found in a relatively small geographic area; it is organized along ethnic lines to the extent that most hustlers are Hispanic while almost all clients are Caucasian; there is a social class dimension; it is an income-producing activity rather than a recreational one; most of the hustlers work in the area and live elsewhere; the market depends to some extent on repeat clients, who either travel through on their way to work or reside in the area; and there are institutions and organizations that either facilitate hustling or provide places where hustlers can gather on their own. The following pages describe the nature of this market and its participants, as well as some of the important events which have affected it.

In addition to the organizational qualities of hustling, perhaps the most important contribution of this study may be to offer a way of thinking about hustling in Times Square. I view the hustlers of Times Square as a community within a structured marketplace. Moreover, the community's existence is due in part to the organizational features of the hustling market. The hustling community is currently being affected by a number of changes taking place in Times Square. Urban redevelopment, the emergence of crack, and an increased impact of AIDS, among other factors, have affected every aspect of hustling in Times Square as well as each member of the population. This project, then, involves a journey into the community of street hustlers in Times Square. The goals are to understand the rhythm and flow of the culture, its shapes and textures, and how the interactions, rituals, and relationships are constructed and understood by its members. This was accomplished by locating a position on the social landscape and allowing this relatively unknown culture to unfold before me. By becoming immersed in this culture, I was able not only to understand "the life," but also to witness firsthand the effects of these community changes.

METHODOLOGICAL ISSUES

This research took place primarily in the Times Square section of New York City, although some occurred elsewhere in the Midtown Manhattan area and in Greenwich Village in lower Manhattan. In collecting these data, I used classic ethnographic methods of direct observation and open-ended, unstructured interviews. From January to December 1992, I spent an average of three to five hours per day, two to three days a week, observing, interviewing and interacting with hustlers. I also interviewed peep show managers, employees, shopkeepers, hotel clerks, and various street people (e.g. drug dealers, con artists, homeless). In part, I designed these interviews to gain access to the population.

GAINING ENTRY

Gaining entry into hard-to-reach populations presents a host of problems for researchers (Luckenbill 1985; Douglas 1972; Karp 1980; Hammersley and Atkinson 1983). Often, the researcher must rely on informants to provide key information about the population as well as providing introductions to its members. Early on in my research, shopkeepers pointed out areas where a good deal of hustling takes place, offered opinions on the nature of the problem, and, in a few cases, introduced me to hustlers. My contacts with other researchers in the area and street people whom I had come to know were also helpful. Through these networks, I was able to interview thirty-five hustlers. Because large segments of the population pride themselves on anonymity, I cannot make a claim about the representativeness of these interviews. However, I feel confident that what "the boys" have told me about the trade, the culture of hustling, and their lives has been accurate and consistent. When possible, I have verified the information through personal observation or by asking my informants or other hustlers for verification. These methods are obviously not without limitations, but they did serve to support the information provided by the boys. Nevertheless, it should be stressed that I am focusing on a select segment of the hustling population in New York City. My insights, assessments, and conclusions can only be applied to the hustlers in Times Square.

One of the most consistent questions people ask about this project, be they scholars or laypersons, is how I made initial contact with the boys. My first encounter with a hustler occurred after I had been in the field for about a month. I spent January making some preliminary observations as well as building a network to gain entrance into the population. I talked with people involved in the sex trade and the Times Square scene and attempted to learn more about the outreach programs in the area.

By February I felt I knew enough about the trade to begin interviewing hustlers. I encountered Eddie on the upper concourse of the Port Authority Bus Terminal. He was dressed in tight jeans, sneakers, and a hooded sweat shirt and was standing next to one of the doorways near the departure gates, a common pickup spot. Twice I saw him greet older men with a short conversation that ended with him shaking his head no. The men would depart and Eddie would remain, seemingly waiting for someone. He would make eye contact with a few passersby and in some cases quietly call out to them as they walked by. While this may appear to the casual observer as innocuous behavior, it led me to believe that Eddie was a hustler. I decided to approach him and determine if my initial assessment was correct: it was.

This was my first interview and I recorded it in my field notes immediately after it occurred. The verbal sparring was typical of the other encounters I had with hustlers who were not introduced to me.

MC: How's it goin'. I'm Bob.

E: I'm Eddie. How ya doin'.

MC: Listen I'm wondering if you could help me out, I'm writing a book about hustlers in Times Square. I was wondering if you knew anybody who hustled and would be willing to talk to me about it.

E: You writin' a book about hustlers? Here? How much?

MC: How much what?

E: How much you payin'?

MC: You don't understand, that's why I need your help. I don't have much money, but I could buy you lunch and we could talk about your experiences here.

E: You wanna what? Buy me lunch? What the hell am I gonna do with that? I can't spend that! You know my time is money, I can't be wastin' it talkin' to you or eatin' lunch.

MC: But you have to eat, right?

E: I'm not hungry.

MC: Okay, then how about I just stand here and hang out with you and ask you some questions until a trick comes along and then you leave?

E: If you stand around here, no tricks will come cause they'll think I'm talkin' to you.

MC: All right, what if you introduced me to some of your friends who hustle who aren't working now. You tell them what I'm doing and that I can't pay cash and basically say I'm okay. Then when you do have time and you are hungry, we can talk some more. That way you don't have to worry about losing money now and you can help out one of your friends who is hungry and who isn't hustling today.

E: So what do I get out of it?

MC: What you get out of it is that you help out one of your friends, you help me, and then the next time I see you, you can help yourself. You aren't always hustling. You have to eat at some point, so let me buy you lunch and all we're going to do is talk. If I ask you something you don't want to answer, then don't. So we would be helping each other and your friends. And if you and I get along, maybe you can introduce me to more of your friends or maybe you and I can hang out sometime. But right now, it doesn't cost you anything and all I want to do is meet other hustlers who aren't working so I can talk to them. After you introduce me and tell them what's up, you're done.

E: And all you want to do is talk? Nothin' else? And you can't pay? Oh, lord, what do I look like, some sort of social worker?

MC: You look like a guy who's smart enough to see what this is about and you are also smart enough to see that this could work out for everybody. You help your friends out and yourself at the same time. So how about it?

E: Okay, but I want to talk to you first. If you writin' a book I want my name in it. But I'm only gonna give you ten minutes. If I like you, I'll help you, but if I don't, I ain't doin' shit. Come on, you can buy me a slice over at that pizza shop.

That interview with Eddie lasted forty-five minutes. From that point on, he introduced me to many of his friends. Once he started talking he never stopped, but getting him to talk to me initially was a crucial step.

Many of my colleagues (and even some of the boys) have expressed surprise at how quickly and thoroughly I was able to gain access to this population. There were three primary reasons for my success. One of the things that helped establish my position in the culture was my willingness to deal with the same adversities the boys faced. They told me I earned their respect because, despite the freezing cold of winter or the sweltering heat of summer, I "hung out" and suffered from the elements along with them.

Moreover, unlike others in their lives, I was interested in what they had to say, did not pass judgment on them or their opinions, and was straightforward from the time of my initial contact with them. This, according to the boys, earned their respect. Prince told me:

> You never dissed [show a lack of respect] us. You always straight up and you listen. You okay man, for a white boy, you okay. Like I never get to tell nobody how I feel about shit, you understand? Things like life and shit. But you, I know you interested in me and what I gots to say, I like that. And most of these other guys like that too. That's why you was accepted so fast. Like I said, you okay as far as I'm concerned. How many people you know will come out here, ask us how we doin', buy us lunch, ask us if we okay and then give us your phone number and say call if we need anything? You ain't really no researcher as far as I'm concerned, you a friend of ours.

While this is indeed speculation on my part, and based largely on my own beliefs and assessment, I think my immersion into the environment was successful in part because I went to the hustlers in their setting instead of having them come to me in mine. I also felt I could not, in good faith, represent myself to be something I was not. The trust that I engendered was tenuous in some instances, but I believe it may have been based on my fulfillment of any promises I made. For example, if I talked to someone on the condition that I would buy him lunch in return or meet him on a certain day to help him with welfare benefits, I felt obliged to show up as promised or else I should not have agreed to help in the first place. I believe they knew this and, as time progressed, they began to trust me and tell me more about themselves. This research approach granted me entrance into a hidden population in Times Square that few researchers have explored in any detail.

I was also very concerned about confidentiality and protecting the hustlers' identities. I applied for, and received, a Certificate of

Confidentiality from the United States Department of Health and Human Services. This provided legal protection for my sources. I made a point of explaining what this document was and how it maintained their anonymity. I also took the added precaution of asking them what they wanted to be called rather than simply using their street names. In some cases, they said it did not matter, but I wanted to be clear about what I was doing and why. These boys appeared indifferent and said their street names could be used. Nonetheless, as an added precaution, in the text I use fictitious names for these individuals.

I also told the boys that I would bring them some of my field notes to read if they were so inclined. Later, I explained, I would also bring the completed chapters along so that they could give me their comments and offer any suggestions or clarifications that they felt were needed. This went a long way toward enhancing my credibility and standing in the community. My offer to share the contents of my work was perceived as an honest attempt to understand their world and learn from them, not to simply extract the information and depart, never to be heard from again.

A second factor in my success with the boys involved my passing a series of tests. For instance, a hustler would share a piece of information with me, make me promise it was to be held in the strictest of confidence, and then wait to see if I mentioned it to anyone else. When I did not, he would tell others that I was trustworthy. Other tests determined if I would uphold my end of an arrangement. Early on, I had established an agreement with the boys that I could not give them cash but would be willing to buy them lunch, cigarettes, or other incidentals in exchange for their time and insight. This was done to offset the income they would forgo by talking to me.

As they came to know and trust me, this issue became moot, and the boys would freely seek me out to tell me the latest news of their lives or what had happened since our last meeting. Our interaction became less an exchange and more a social relationship. I still purchased incidentals or lunch for them, but I would usually bring the subject up by asking a boy if he had eaten that day.

To test my resolve as well as their ability to "work" me, some hustlers would occasionally ask for a dollar or two to buy groceries for their family. I would remind them of our understanding, and, in turn, they would try to play on my sympathies. One parrying tactic I used was to offer to buy groceries for them and to have them take me to meet their "incredibly beautiful but hungry baby."

The point in all the tests or attempted scams was to determine whether I would make exceptions to our agreement. If I wavered even once, a precedent would be set and a deluge of requests might follow. Moreover, my standing in the community would be damaged: I could be "played." Knowing this, I remained steadfast in my position. As it turns out, this was the correct response. Within a short time, perhaps three or four months into the project, the tests had all but stopped. Occasionally a hustler reintroduced one, but it was usually a playful attempt, performed more as a joke coupled with a reminder of how the hustlers had "tested" me in the past.

Perhaps most important, the project benefited greatly from the active interest of three individuals. Since they played leadership roles within the culture, my association with them was critical. Their introductions to other hustlers not only paved the way for those particular interviews, the effect snowballed and additional introductions came at a relatively rapid pace. These three hustlers became my cultural guides, pointing out new developments, providing and verifying information about others in the trade, and making important contacts for me. Although I will describe them in greater detail in the next chapter, they merit a cursory introduction here. Flacco is thirty years old. He has been involved in the Times Square scene for nearly seventeen years and his time spent there accords him respect by the other hustlers. Many come to him for advice and counsel when they are in need. Apache, who is twenty-one, has only seven years of experience in the trade. However, he possesses intelligence and business acumen far beyond his years or his tenth grade education. Since he is wise to the various street scams and possesses excellent powers of reasoning, he, too, commands respect within the culture. Finally, Raul, at twenty-eight, is bigger, stronger, and more tempestuous than most hustlers and therefore serves in a protector role for many people. His status is derived from intimidation and fear. As he is fond of saying, he never met a fight he didn't like.

OBSERVATIONS

I have come to know many hustlers in the area and have had numerous conversations with them, often in pairs or groups. I spent a great deal of time simply hanging out and observing their behavior, rituals, and activities. These observations occurred in a variety of places including coffee shops, fastfood restaurants, street corners, bars, and parks. A favorite pastime for the boys is to play handball in the nearby parks. The games are competitive and I learned a great deal about the boys by simply observing the games and how the players interacted. Some of the most interesting observations involved the dynamics of the transaction between the boys and their clients. Many of these took place on 42nd Street and 8th Avenue, especially in front of the peep shows.

INTERVIEWS

In order to learn as much about the boys as possible and to best understand their environment, I used a life history approach. Life histories can offer insight into a subject, including the individual's life situation and the state of the world, as he or she understands it, either at some particular point in time or over a long period. The interviews were of two basic types. One was a conversational interview in which there was no agenda and the subject controlled the flow and topic of conversation. The other type, while related to the first in that it was still open-ended, involved a general set of topics in which I guided the interview. In each type of interview, as well as in the informal conversations, I tried to get a sense of the boy's personal background, life style, relationships with others, and perceptions of how hustling has changed in recent times, as well as measures he took to adapt to these changes.

While I tried to understand the boys and their world, I made no attempt to fit an explanatory structure into the culture. I had no stated hypotheses, no theories to test. Rather, armed only with my "sociological hunting license" and an inexhaustible curiosity, I ventured into the field to learn something about the 42nd Street scene and the people who make their living there.

PROBLEMS AND SOLUTIONS IN THE FIELD

Despite my acceptance into the culture, I encountered difficulty from some hustlers who did not believe what they had heard about me. In an effort to remedy this, I often carried economy-sized packs of chewing gum, which I offered to those I knew and those I had just met. It was a great icebreaker and allowed me to inform them that I was simply trying to write about their lives. As time went on, my acquaintance with other hustlers served as a legitimizing mechanism. That is, my credibility was enhanced by having already talked to people the skeptics knew.

An obvious potential problem in working with this population was my personal safety. While I was accepted by most hustlers, who evinced a sense of responsibility for my safety, I could not rely on them completely in the event of trouble. One precautionary strategy that I adopted was to call home on an hourly basis. I also sent letters to the Port Authority Police and the mayor's Office of Midtown Enforcement explaining who I was and that I was conducting social science research in the area. I also explained that as a security precaution I would be checking in periodically at home and that if anything went wrong, my wife would contact their office with my description and last known location.

Whenever I arrived in Times Square, I would check in and tell my wife where I was and where I would be going during the next hour. An hour or so later, I would call and tell her where I was going next. If I did not check in within a two hour period, she was to call the police. I gave myself a two hour cushion in the event I could not easily break away to call, such as during a very personal or emotional interview with one of the boys. This was not a strategy without limitations and there were a few instances where I came extremely close to violating the two hour limit. Fortunately, my wife understood the difficulties of field research and remained calm. Interestingly, my informants understood my purpose in checking in and even reminded me to "go check in" on a few occasions. They would then explain my brief absence to others who might not know why I left.

Another problem that I confronted was my role in the culture. In deviant populations, members must always keep a wary eye out for the police, particularly undercover officers. This is especially true in Times Square, where the Port Authority Police as well as the New York City Police Department have escalated their undercover "sting" operations. As a result, strangers are given a great deal of scrutiny.

One problem in researching this population is that there are very few roles that an adult male can play. Essentially, one is perceived as either a client, a police officer, a commuter or "suit," or in some cases, an older hustler. Since I purposely avoided dressing like a "fly Puerto Rican," [hip, in style] the latter possibility was quickly eliminated. The role of researcher was not at all defined.

Many of the boys stated that they initially thought I was a police officer. They sensed something about my presentation of self, or in their words, I "smelled like a cop." There may be some accuracy to this assessment since I had six years experience as a security officer as well as some law enforcement training. In many ways, I may have indeed "smelled" like a police officer. Others thought I was a client, especially when they saw me talking to many different hustlers.

I had a few encounters in which one hustler propositioned me in front of another, which set off a round of arguments and angry threats. This occurred for two primary reasons. One was the aforementioned sense of responsibility my informants felt for my safety, while the other reason has to do with the normative system that regulates the boys' behavior. In either case, my role was not at all clear. Eventually, the word spread that I was writing a book about hustlers in Times Square and my place in the neighborhood became understood and accepted.

This role was carefully constructed for the reasons I just outlined. I needed to maintain a sense of distinction and separation so that others who did not know me would be able to understand who I was without cause for concern. I wanted to be part of the culture, but at the same time I needed a certain objective distance in order for my presence to be understood as well as to prevent my "going native." This role separation is a concept that Hammersley and Atkinson (1983) and Agar (1980) have discussed at length.

How I dressed played a very important role, especially early in the course of the project. While some researchers might find themselves thinking about how to dress like the natives lest they be identified as outsiders, I had the somewhat difficult task of trying to dress differently. This was especially important since I did not want to be mistaken for an undercover police officer. Had I tried to dress like a hustler, I would have certainly been identified as a police officer, and if I dressed as I normally did, I would also be identified as one. The boys felt that white men, especially white men in their early to late thirties, who wore untucked tennis shirts and various sports-related clothing such as National Football League (NFL) jackets or hats, had various bulges around the waistband, and spent a lot of time standing around watching people, were cops. This made it very difficult to gain entry into the population. Here again, my informants played a key role. After I got to know them, they legitimized my presence by introducing me to other hustlers. Consequently, early on in the project I spent almost all my time with either Raul, Apache, or Flacco.

Finally, my relationship with outside agencies played a role within the culture. At the beginning of the project, I contacted some of the various outreach programs such as Covenant House, Streetworks Project, the Door, and Project Return. Due to problems stemming from client confidentiality, they rejected my requests to interview workers or any of the youths. However, what I thought initially would be an obstacle turned into an advantage as I became known in the hustling population. A few boys asked me if I was or had been affiliated with such groups. When they found that I was not, my credibility actually increased. This was especially true after I told them that the organizations had refused to help me.

It seems there is a good deal of animosity between some of these programs and many hustlers. While a few individuals will take advantage of the resources the programs offer, most want little to do with them or their staff. The fact that the agencies would not help me served as a bond between us. This was especially true of Covenant House, an organization for which most of the boys have a particular distaste. This is due largely to its rigid behavior code for clients.

I did have a few opportunities to learn about the programs from the inside, however. Apache, who was ever the enterprising soul, would occasionally go to Streetworks Project for groceries, and he simply brought me along and told everyone he wanted me there. Since I was accompanied by someone who was using the Project's services, I was allowed access.

These are a few of the more problematic issues that I faced in my attempt to become a part of this population. In the following pages, I would like to tell you the boys' story and describe how hustling has changed dramatically in recent times. Since the boys capture the essence of a hustler's life, wherever possible I let them speak for themselves and tell their story in their own words.

The next chapter sets the stage, describing a bit of the history of Times Square as well as the people and features of what is referred to as "the bright light zone." Chapter 3 introduces the principal characters. The scene is Times Square, but the hub of hustling involves the areas of 42nd Street and 8th Avenue. Chapter 4 discusses the nature of the trade through a typical day in the life of a young male prostitute. In the context of these three chapters, the characteristics of the hustling market are described in greater detail.

Chapter 5 marks a dramatic change in the culture: the widespread use of crack. Chapter 6 talks about the risks associated with AIDS and how the boys accommodate and cope with these risks. Chapter 7 describes how civic changes, urban redevelopment, and law enforcement strategies have caused the locale of the hustling market to shift. These last three chapters are central to the study as well as to an overall understanding of the dynamics of the culture. I will offer some sociological insights into these three events and their impact on the community. In one sense, it may be the case that what is currently seen as hustling is fading from the Times Square scene and that, in a way, this study may have caught glimpses of a disintegrating culture.

Finally, in chapter 8, I update the status and situation of some of the boys, discussing where they are now and what they are doing, and offer a few comments on the direction in which this population, the market, and the "occupation" are headed.

REFERENCES

Agar, Michael. 1980. *The Professional Stranger*. New York: Academic Press Inc.

Borus-Rotheram, Mary, and Cheryl Koopman. 1991. "Sexual Risk Behaviors, AIDS Knowledge and Beliefs about AIDS among Runaways." *American Journal of Public Health* 81(2):206-208.

Bracey, Dorothy. 1989. *Baby Pros: Adolescent Prostitution*. New York: John Jay Press.

Butts, William Marlin. 1947. "Boy Prostitutes of the Metropolis." *Journal of Clinical Psychopathology* 8:673-681.

Calhoun, Thomas, and Brian Pickerill. 1988. "Young Male Prostitutes: Their Knowledge of Selected Sexually Transmitted Diseases." *Psychology: A Journal of Human Behavior* 25(3/4):1-8.

Campagna, Daniel J., and Donald L. Poffenberger. 1988. *The Sexual Trafficking of Children*. South Hadley, Mass.: Auburn House.

Coombs, Neil. 1974. "Male Prostitution: A Psychological View of Behavior." *American Journal of Orthopsychiatry* 44(5):782-789.

Douglas, Jack. 1972. *Research on Deviants*. Beverly Hills, Calif.: Sage Publications.

Drew, Dennis, and Jonathan Drake. 1969. *Boys for Sale*. New York: Brown Book Company.

Elifson, Kurt, Jacqueline Boles, and Michael Sweat. 1993. "Risk Factors Associated with HIV Infection Among Male Prostitutes." *American Journal of Public Health* 83:79-83.

Hammersley, Martyn and Paul Atkinson. 1983. *Ethnography: Principles and Practices*. London: Tavistock.

James, Jennifer. 1982. *Entrance into Male Prostitution.* Washington D.C.: The National Institute of Mental Health.

Jersild, Jens. 1956. *Boy Prostitution.* Copenhagen, Denmark: C. E. Gad.

Karp, D.A. 1980. "Observing Behavior in Public Places: Problems and Strategies." in W.B. Shaffir, R.A. Stebbins and A. Turowetz eds. *Fieldwork Experience: Qualitative Approaches to Social Research.* New York: St. Martin's Press.

Lauderback, David, and Donald Waldorf. 1989. "Male Prostitution and AIDS: Preliminary Findings." *Focus: A Guide to AIDS Research* Jan. 3-4.

Lloyd, Robin. 1976. *For Money or Love.* New York: The Free Press.

Luckenbill, David. 1985. "Dynamics of the Deviant Sale." *Deviant Behavior* 5(1):131-51.

Luckenbill, David. 1986a. "Deviant Career Mobility: The Case of Male Prostitution." *Social Problems* 33(4):283-96.

Luckenbill, David. 1986b. "Entering Male Prostitution." *Urban Life* 14(2):131-53.

MacNamara, Donal E.J. 1965. "Male Prostitution in American Cities: A Socioeconomic or Pathological Phenomenon?" *American Journal of Orthopsychiatry* 35:204.

Morse, Edward, Patricia Simon, Howard Osofsky, Paul Balson, and Richard Gaumer. 1991. "The Male Street Prostitute: A Vector for Transmission of HIV Infection into the Heterosexual World." *Social Science and Medicine* 32(5):535.

Pleak, Richard R., and Heino Meyer-Bahlburg. 1990. "Sexual Behavior and AIDS Knowledge of Young Male Prostitutes in Manhattan." *Journal of Sex Research* 27(4):557-587.

Reiss, Albert J., Jr. 1961. "The Social Integration of Queers and Peers." *Social Problems* 9(2):102-20.

Ross, Laurence H. 1959. "The Hustler in Chicago." *Journal of Student Research* 1:13-19.

Ross, Michael. 1988. "Social and Behavioral Aspects of Male Homosexuals." *The Medical Clinics of North America* 70(3):537-47.

Weisberg, Kelly D. 1985. *Children of the Night.* South Hadley, Mass.: Lexington Books.

West, Donald J. 1991. *Male Prostitution.* New York: Harrington Park Press.

2

The Scene

For more than sixty years, Times Square has reigned as one of New York's premier tourist attractions. Recent times have brought an annual average twenty million American and foreign tourists to visit New York City, and Times Square is a sight that most do not miss (Bloom 1991). Running from 6th to 8th Avenues and from 40th Street to 53rd, the square has traditionally represented the variety of entertainment for which New York is famous (see Map 2.1). Those with a flair for the dramatic are drawn by Broadway and the theater district. Almost eight million patrons of the theater support over 20,000 jobs and spend an estimated $750 million each year, thus playing an important role in the Times Square scene (Bloom 1991). However, the dramatic arts are not all the area offers.

For those who have a preference for pop or contemporary culture, there are movie houses, arcades, restaurants, and bars, while the area of the 42nd Street corridor and 8th Avenue, with its own brand of bawdy entertainment and erotically exciting street life, appeals to those who are attracted to titillating offerings.

Times Square is also one of New York's most active transportation centers. The 7th Avenue station of the IRT subway line, the 8th Avenue station of the IND line, and the Times Square BMT line, all on 42nd Street, are the busiest in the city. According to the Mass Transit Authority, in 1991 approximately 200,000 people used these two subway stations daily. The Port Authority Bus Terminal, which is located on 8th Avenue and 42nd Street, brings another 185,000 people to the area each day. Most are commuters, but the number of people attracted to the area for the theater and other forms of entertainment is also substantial.

·MAP OF TIMES SQUARE·

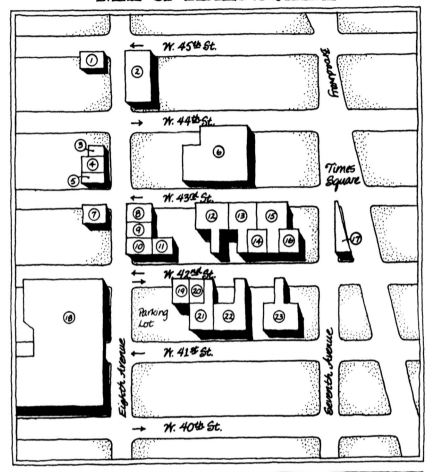

1. Beefsteak Charlie's
2. Milford Plaza Hotel
3. Cameo Cinema
4. Club 44
5. Adonis Theater
6. N.Y. Times Bldg.
7. Show World Center
8. All Male Revue
9. Show Palace
10. King's Famous Fried Chicken & Mexican Café
11. Harem Theater
12. Selwyn Theater
13. Academy Theater
14. Times Square Theater
15. Lyric Theater
16. Victory Theater
17. Newsday Bldg.
18. Port Authority Bus Terminal
19. Joy & Roxy Theaters
20. Peepland
21. Liberty Theater
22. Harris Theater
23. New Amsterdam Theater

Times Square is the only spot where the hundreds of different worlds that comprise New York City meet face to face. It brings together Broadway stars, tourists, passersby, prostitutes, drug dealers, and a host of other individuals with funny, dramatic, and sometimes deadly results. Thus, Times Square exemplifies New York's admiration of diversity: in just a few blocks filled with bright lights and social stimulation there exists a happy frenzy of night life, theater bliss, and the spontaneous "razzmatazz" of the Rialto.

Additionally, Times Square serves as a meeting place for events of significant social importance. Few New Yorkers can imagine a New Year's Eve without the ceremonial dropping of the ball at midnight, and many will fondly remember the square as the site of jubilation over American victories of world conflict. Times Square serves as a symbol for New Yorkers—one with a variety of meanings, but nevertheless, one with long-standing traditions. Its history as an entertainment district has played an integral role in shaping its present and future.

THE OLD STAGE

While the history of Times Square dates back to the Revolutionary War, when General George Washington and his troops occupied sites on what is now Bryant Park, the period of transition began during the early 1800s when the area was home to squatters who settled along the creek known as Great Kill. The stream was later filled in and became 42nd Street; it was used as a manure dump site during the nineteenth Century (Bloom 1991).

However, the nineteenth Century was an era of modernization for Times Square, as symbolized by the construction of numerous theaters: there were eighty by 1895. Along with this development came great wealth for the owners, such as Hammerstein, Zigfield, Ochs, and T. Henry French, who built the first theater on 42nd Street, the American. Most of the successful theaters were owned by a group of investors known as the Shubert Brothers. During the late 1800s, New Yorkers spent an estimated six million dollars per year on entertainment. Additionally, the area along Broadway from 37th and 42nd Streets was named "the Rialto" (Bloom 1991).

The solidification of the square came in the early 1900s, when real estate values skyrocketed. New construction on Broadway widened the street from 34th to 59th Street and brought it across Seventh Avenue at 42nd Street, creating the now famous Crossroads Block and the Great White Way. In 1904, the Times Tower, the new headquarters of the *New York Times*, was built on this triangular block. In tribute to the newspaper, the area once known as Longacre Square (named for the famous carriage manufacturer in England) was renamed Times Square (Erenberg 1981).

The area continued to grow as a focal point of the city: it was used for rallies to sell war bonds, political demonstrations, and parades, and of course, the first ball was dropped on New Year's Eve 1908. As the success of the area as a social gathering place increased, the *New York Times* constructed the now-famous zipper sign around the building in 1928, allowing the paper to bring the news to a street audience. Although the Times has since relocated to 43rd Street, the building remains a fixture in the area (Bloom 1991).

During the 1920s, Prohibition dealt a serious blow to the entertainment industry as abstinence laws forced many theaters and night clubs to close. At approximately the same time, due in part to the development of mass transit in the area, real estate values underwent an explosive upturn, which forced many theater owners to double, or even triple, their ticket prices. Higher prices, increased competition, and the development and popularity of radio forced many of the theaters in Times Square to either convert to burlesque shows, to close, or to provide these new forms of entertainment to customers. However, even the burlesque shows and other forms of live entertainment were short-lived. Technology and the stock market crash of 1929 irrevocably changed Times Square.

Theaters then began showing pornographic films, commonly called "grind flicks," because of the number of times a movie could be shown during the course of a single day. However, the nickname today has a different meaning akin to the phrase "bump and grind," which was formerly used to describe the dancers in burlesque houses. The area continued its slide into the seedy and unsavory. The runaway and vagrant population grew, largely due to the opening of the Port Authority Bus Terminal in 1950, and areas of 42nd Street (known as "The Deuce"), and 8th Avenue became a haven for criminals (Kornblum and Williams 1994).

The late 1970s and 1980s offered the area no relief from the deterioration and Times Square became a chaotic scene of drugs, sex, and crime. The Deuce and 8th Avenue became a no-man's-land of the crack trade. Amid the denizens of porn palaces, con men, hookers, drug dealers, and muggers, Times Square's fall into disrepute reached its nadir. The *New York Post* wrote in 1984: "Crime, drug abuse, pornography, prostitution all flourish in Times Square. What was once the premier tourist attraction of the world, the heart and soul of New York City, is a squalid collection of dilapidated and deteriorated buildings." What was once the gleaming pride of New York City became an embarrassment, a festering wound that showed no signs of healing. Crime was out of control in this part of the city. According to the mayor's Office of Midtown Enforcement, in 1988, 2,246 crimes were reported to the police on the 42nd Street block between 7th and 8th Avenues, more than on any other single block in New York City. Part I or index crimes, which are considered the most serious offenses, comprised almost 30% of the total. In 1989, the problem grew worse with 2,309 crimes reported, more than in any other year in recent history. Moreover, 44% of these crimes were Part I offenses. Thus, seeking thrills and excitement in Times Square became an even more dangerous proposition.

Today Times Square continues to be a brassy and dangerous place. The precipitous fall from glamour has brought with it a host of undesirables and an increased potential for violence and conflict. The danger in a place like Times Square is very real and omnipresent.

* * * *

As I walk from Grand Central Station toward West 42nd Street, I find no traces of the sex trade until I approach 6th Avenue. Numerous business people, secretaries, students, mothers, and shoppers can be found in and around the area. Lovers walk hand in hand, dodging traffic in their attempt to reach the sanctuary of Bryant Park, only a short distance away. About a third of the way down the block, I discover two peep shows on either side of 42nd Street. The remaining buildings consist of banks, luggage shops, a number of electronics stores, shoe stores, pizza places, sporting goods stores, and a boxing gym near Broadway. These peep shows seem anomalous in an otherwise typical Manhattan street. As one approaches them, one gets the initial impression that they are out of place, somehow disjointed in the rhythm of the area. That impression changes after time spent watching the people who go into these shops. The steady stream coming and going, consisting mostly of middle-aged men, is as much a part of the heartbeat of this area as anything else.

As I make my way to Broadway and the Crossroads Block, the *New York Newsday* building's zipper sign tells me the time, the temperature, and the leading headline of today—another story of a white police officer shooting a black youth, this time in the Washington Heights section of the city. On the opposite side of the street is the Traveler's Arch. At one time it was both a tourist information center and a police substation, but now it serves instead as the resting place for homeless men and women who sit on the steps and eat, sleep, argue, or chat with their associates. Today many homeless men, who appear comfortable in their place of respite, remain, drifting off to sleep.

A large, overweight man, aged approximately forty and balding on top but managing a thin, gray ponytail in back, and looking considerably worn, has been sitting on the steps and now attempts to stand. The sneakers he is wearing are torn and the laces are missing. His green plaid pants are worn thin from constant use and have several large grease stains near the knees and thighs. As he attempts to stand on the steps he loses his balance and falls toward the concrete, landing on a soundly sleeping homeless man who has almost missed the comical display of coordination. Unfortunately, the first man falls face-first into the second man's groin. I clearly hear shrieks from both men over the sounds of the passing vehicles and the murmur of conversations among the passersby. So loud are the cries that some people momentarily stop and attempt to locate the source.

Both men lumber to their feet and a standoff occurs, with the two shouting insults and vulgarities at one another. Part of the anger of the first man appears to stem from the embarrassment of finding his face in another man's crotch. As the men stand on the steps shouting, I decide to make my way over to the chess and backgammon players located just around the corner. I cross 42nd Street by the *Newsday* building and make it to the other side just in time to have the misfortune of being caught in the middle of the ensuing brawl. I have no time to dodge the two shabby-looking combatants, both of whom are headed on a collision course toward me.

The second man, still slowed from the blow to the groin, wrestles his opponent down, and both crash into me, taking me right off my feet. In a moment's time, I am being rolled on by two foul-smelling and angry men, placing me literally on the bottom of a three man pile.

My commands and pleas go unheeded. Finally, I untangle one leg for long enough to thrash out and it catches the second man's groin. He again howls in pain and rolls off. I manage to get to my feet and push my way past the crowd of people that had gathered. In one sense, I was glad a group had collected since it gave me an escape route. A little disheveled and embarrassed, I dust myself off, laugh a bit at my bad timing, and continue down 42nd Street.

THE NEW STAGE

A stroll down this street reveals much of the history and fame of Times Square. The architectural style of the buildings and theaters is a constant reminder of what was once one of the most active entertainment centers in the country. Today a total of nine theaters remain on this street, but only three are open for business. One has been converted to a pornographic (porno) video store, while the other two show first-run feature films. At one time the prices for these movies were less than elsewhere in the city, but times have changed and customers from all over the city who used to frequent these cinemas can no longer afford to do so. Today, the theaters instead provide a meeting place for hustlers who have earned enough money for the day and want to take a girlfriend out or spend time with friends, or for those who simply wish to kill time between tricks.

A cursory view of the corridor also reveals the effects of the 42nd Street Development Project. This project, one of the most elaborate efforts since the construction of the Rockefeller Center, calls for the construction of four office towers at 42nd Street and Broadway, and at 8th Avenue, a huge market and a 750-room hotel. Moreover, seven theaters along 42nd Street will be renovated, along with the area's subway stations. The city plans to purchase or condemn the entire block between 7th and 8th Avenues and then turn it over to developers for reconstruction. The political and legal battles have finally ended, yet the economic climate has caused developers to suspend construction of the towers (Dunlap 1990). The only signs of redevelopment are the now-familiar blue plywood boards marked ''Post No Bills'' in white, stenciled letters that cover what used to be many storefronts.

Of the fifty-six businesses on the street, only thirty-three remain open. Similar to the portion of 42nd Street near 5th and 6th Avenues described earlier, these shops consist of restaurants, sporting goods stores, electronic shops, delicatessens, and convenience stores, mixed in with the theaters. Of the thirty-three active businesses, sixteen, just less than half, are sex related. These include the actual peep shows, such as Playland, Peepland, and Roxy, as well as stores that sell porno video tapes. The latter are extremely lucrative ventures, but the competition is fierce.

Almost all the stores employ "barkers" or "steerers" to stand outside the shops and entice passersby to peruse their merchandise. They also pass out pamphlets to anyone willing to accept them. Many of the barkers are quick to point out their resourcefulness to anyone who seems interested. If a person wants something other than video tapes, they are willing and able to procure drugs, live companionship, or anything else he/she desires.

Of the closed businesses, it appears that only three or four were porno related. The majority were either fast-food restaurants or accessories stores, such as those selling jewelry and other novelties. All these shops are located at the ground level of other, much larger buildings. The same is true for the shops that remain open, which often seem to be the only source of life in many of the buildings. The upper floors are lifeless and dark, and the dust and obvious emptiness indicates they have not been occupied for some time.

Other buildings are burned out in the upper floors, perhaps the result of an enterprising landlord hoping to capitalize on an insurance claim. Were it not for the storefront operations and the few remaining theaters, 42nd Street would be devoid of any real activity except perhaps as a shortcut for commuters on their way to the Port Authority Bus Terminal.

Recently there has been a noticeable change in the street's activity. There are not nearly as many street hustlers or anyone else for that matter. This is due partly to the visible police presence up and down 42nd Street, and partly to the closing of so many sex-related businesses. Crime has also been reduced. According to the mayor's Office of Midtown Enforcement, in 1991, for example, there were 1,073 reported crimes on the street, an overall decrease of 54% from 1989. Part II offenses such as simple assault, purse snatching, criminal mischief, and petty larceny, were down 64%, while Part I crimes, especially robberies, were down 36%.

Most of the criminal activity occurs at the west end of the street, where it intersects with 8th Avenue. On the right just before the King's Famous Fried Chicken and Mexican Cafe, there is an alleyway that often goes unnoticed. Farther in, a staircase leads to a subway entrance.

Prior to the subway entry there is a long hallway with a small arcade to the right. The arcade consists of a half dozen machines, mostly pinball games, all of which are in various states of repair or abuse. In this dank, urine-smelling corridor, a great deal of drug-related activities occur. Dealers stand to one side of the hallway quietly selling their wares, empty crack vials crunch underfoot, and users sitting on the steps or against the wall gaze up at passersby through a drug-induced reverie. The smell of crack is very strong and a blue cloud of smoke fills the confined area, causing those who enter to feel the drug's effects as well.

Everyone who passes through this hallway is scrutinized with great care by the dealers and less closely by the users. However, the paranoia that many crack users experience after smoking the drug, especially in such a confined space, can be very dangerous. White men are of particular concern since they are often "made for" [identified as] police officers. Since this area is so close to the Port Authority Bus Terminal as well as the action on 8th Avenue, it attracts many hustlers, users, and of course, the police. After even an hour or two spent observing, it is common to see undercover officers escorting a handcuffed individual from the alley.

Directly across the street is a large parking lot. While one might assume that this type of business would help quell the amount of crime in the general area, it is actually one of the most active crime spots in Times Square and is frequented by men who loiter, murmuring comments to passersby such as: "AT&T, MCI, I got what you need man. Tell me what you need, you call anywhere in the world for ten minutes, I only charge you $25." This is the world of the phone hustler or phone card thief.

As many as thirty people, all of whom have stolen telephone credit cards and are trying to sell time on them as quickly as possible, congregate around this area. On weekends, the number of buyers and sellers multiplies threefold or more. While this is a prime location for this type of activity, there are only four pay phones on the corner. Regardless, there are three primary reasons for this corner's success.

First, the number of people who pass this corner every day runs in the tens of thousands. Second, a tradition of sorts has been established. This is where the market is. While time on stolen credit cards can be found in most areas of the city, the best prices in town can be found here, largely due to the intense competition. Third, the card thieves, most of whom spend their entire day at this location, have the convenience of a deli, the subway, and a ready supply of drugs and sex, all within steps of their work environment. Everything they want or need is within a half block or less.

Eighth Avenue is very similar to 42nd Street but differs in a few ways. First, the redevelopment effort has not affected this street, so there are more businesses. While most people look on 42nd Street and 8th Avenue as the heart of the sex zone in Times Square, there are only nine sex-related businesses from 42nd Street to 46th Street along 8th Avenue. These include peep shows, porno video shops, movie theaters, and strip clubs. Five of these businesses are located between 42nd and 43rd Streets, and of these, Show World Center, the Show Palace, and the All Male Review are perhaps the busiest shops in Times Square.

The Show Palace is one of the most lucrative locations for hustlers to conduct business. The homosexual section of the store is located in the basement and offers privacy for its patrons. Upon entry into this section, which resembles a long rectangle which the patron enters at the lower righthand corner, there are two aisles that offer movies, magazines, and other assorted accessories. A raised counter, similar to a judge's bench, is located near the upper righthand corner but closer to the center. A hallway divides two rows of video booths running behind this counter and along the entire wall.

The area is kept extremely dark, ostensibly to allow clearer viewing of the monitors in the booths. Each booth has a bench for the patron to sit on which also folds up and out of the way should he wish to stand while watching the movie. The entire booth is constructed of formica, inside and out, for greater durability and easier cleaning. The monitor has a menu on the screen from which the patron selects one of several different movies.

A metal slot accepts only quarters, in receipt of which will provide a few minutes of viewing pleasure. The booths are extremely small, but I have seen two or even three people squeeze their way into a single cubicle. A guard is always posted at one end of the hallway to prevent any sexual or other illegal activities from occurring. Another employee's sole function is to make change for those who run out of quarters, while a third sits in the raised booth and handles the cash register for those who purchase literature, accessories, or movies. Outside Show Palace a number of young males can almost always be found, socializing or looking for prospective clients. The All Male

Review, a live show, provides an additional source of income for hustlers since many clients come to watch the show.

The section between 43rd and 44th Streets on 8th Avenue is also very active. Here there are three sex-related businesses, including the Adonis Theater, an adult video store, and Club 44. Moreover, hustlers and female prostitutes either take their clients to the nearby Meridien Hotel or, in some cases, live there. Along with the Meridien, a number of other hotels in the area serve a similar function including the Sheraton and the Hotel Fulton.

Interspersed with these sex-related shops are a host of fast-food places, grocery and discount stores, pool halls, army/navy stores, and one-hour photo shops. The Milford Plaza, one of New York's more reputable hotels, is located between 44th and 45th Street. All along the street, especially on the corners, are drug dealers, prostitutes, both male and female, and a cast of illegal actors.

Beyond 46th or 48th Streets, the sex scene essentially dies out. Of the fifty-four businesses within the four blocks along 8th Avenue, only twelve are involved in the sex trade. Restaurant Row, one of the most famous regions in New York City, is located on 46th Street. Moreover, the theater district, which is heralded to be the most popular area of entertainment in the city, is only a few blocks away. Ironically, the best and the worst that New York has to offer can be found within a three-block area.

At the other end of 8th Avenue, between 41st and 42nd Streets, is the Port Authority Bus Terminal. Spanning two city blocks, it is one of the most important terminals in all New York City. Inside there are a host of fast food shops, restaurants, book stores, and gift shops, all catering to the needs of travellers. There is even a bowling alley and an arcade for those who have a lot of time to kill between trips or or a burning need to bowl a few frames. It is also a paradise for hustlers. As will become clear in subsequent pages, the Port Authority is central to the lives of hustlers in the area.

THE CAST OF TIMES SQUARE

The people of 42nd Street and 8th Avenue make up a substantial part of its atmosphere. To understand the 42nd Street scene, one needs to know a little about the people and the roles they play. To an outsider walking down this street, it would appear that many people are standing around. Some appear to be waiting, whether for someone or something, and to some extent, this is indeed the case. Some of the roles that inhabitants play are relatively easy to identify. For instance, outside many of the shops, especially those that have sidewalk displays, employees stand near the street and attempt to prevent shoplifting. This is a serious problem for merchants who sell what I call "street accessories," such as baseball hats, driving gloves, and sunglasses. These accoutrements have an important meaning in street life since they contribute to looking fly and thus are in high demand.

Another related role on the street belongs to the owners, managers, or employees of the electronics stores. As there are many of these stores in the area, competition is intense. Consequently, the stores have large window displays and use a variety of marketing techniques, ranging from neon pink signs next to the items, advertising "insanely" low prices, to flashing red lights and sirens.

A cardinal rule among employees of these shops is that once window shoppers enter the foyer to browse the merchandise, they must be lured into the store. The idea is that if the merchant can get them inside, there is a greater chance of making a sale. As a result, many merchants stand outside their shops, and as window shoppers arrive, commence a high-pressure sales pitch. Intermingled with shopkeepers trying to make a sale and avoid a loss of inventory are the barkers for the video stores. At times they shout their prices or noteworthy aspects of their wares, while at other times they pass out coupons or brochures to entice customers.

Smalltime drug dealers are also a common feature of the landscape. Some discreetly offer passersby free samples of their wares, while at other times they do little more than call out the name of the drug. Most attempt to make eye contact with the prospect and then state what they have. If the customer is uninterested, the dealer will often walk along with them and continue to attempt to sell to them.

Walking down 42nd Street and 8th Avenue, then, one is bombarded at almost every point by hawkers of various shapes and sizes: the phone card scammers who pursue an aggressive marketing strategy, drug dealers, and even the security people who are there to prevent shoplifting also engage in a bit of street marketing. However, these are not the only actors in this setting.

Along with these individuals are others who, while physically less harmful, are an integral part of the 42nd Street scene: homeless men and women dot the landscape. Although fewer than in recent times, those who remain make their presence known by asking for spare change. Some will even make a crude but polite sign stating their situation and asking for help. In some cases, a man may state or write (or both) that he is a Vietnam War veteran or an AIDS victim in desperate need of help. A number of men drifting into and out of consciousness post a sign in front of them while they sit on the sidewalk leaning against a building. On the corner of 42nd Street and 8th Avenue, ''god squatters'' often gather just behind the phone card artists against the parking lot fence. This group is made up of a variety of individuals, usually all from the same Christian congregation, who obtain a permit to carry a religious message to the people of 42nd Street. Equipped with a portable loudspeaker and, at times, a cassette player, these men preach peace and the word of God and urge others to find Christ ''while there is still time.''

Vendors are another part of the scenery. The ubiquitous push cart vendors, who sell hot-dogs, pretzels, roast chestnuts, and beef kabobs are as much a staple of this area as anything else I have described thus far. The smells emanating from these carts, especially the smell of chestnuts roasting, for a brief moment allow a breath of serenity into this setting. The vendors endure the oppressive heat and bitter cold of the seasons without complaint and are grateful to have the opportunity to chat with a customer now and then.

Like the vendors in some respects, Muslims set up card tables and sell incense, perfumes, and religious literature under the awnings of closed theaters. These individuals dress in white robes, say very little to entice customers, and often go unmolested by the natives. In addition to these characters of various types, police officers can be seen either walking their beat or passing by on horseback. Additionally, there are late commuters rushing to make their bus, and tourists, complete with their bags from Macys or Bloomingdales and other evidence of the day's efforts, who want to capture some of the excitement and allure of the 42nd Street scene. The sounds and smells, like those in most major cities, are usually loud and foul. The traffic at the intersection of 42nd Street and 8th Avenue is almost always congested, regardless of the time of day. The cacophony of horns from cabs, tractor trailers, and other vehicles, is common. Angered by a slow response or a lapse in traffic etiquette, drivers scream obscenities at each other. These exchanges include comments about each other's position on the evolutionary scale or ethnic background, and gestures underscore the points. Moreover, the odors of exhaust fumes, burning rubber, diesel, and antifreeze coupled with the scents of commuters' sweat and toiletries is a central feature of the area, especially at rush hour. Rush hour in this area has a character all its own. Virtually everyone heads in the same direction: to the Port Authority Bus Terminal. The vast majority of pedestrians move west on 42nd Street from uptown, while a substantial number also head south from the upper 50s along 8th Avenue. Both groups converge on the corners of the intersection. At this point, traffic is completely blocked because the mass of humanity blocks vehicles in almost every direction. As the lights change, a few vehicles caught in the middle of the intersection exacerbate the congestion. To attempt to walk counter to these groups of rush hour commuters and vehicles, is a stifling experience.

TIMES SQUARE'S OTHER FACE

These are some of the people, sounds, and experiences of the street. To look at the scene initially, the activities seem scattered and disjointed. However, there is an underlying structure to the street and the surrounding areas, and the participants understand their roles and the roles of others in the community. There are territorial boundaries and a normative system that dictates a certain etiquette in people's work relationships.

As the sun sets on Times Square, the activities and the level of excitement dramatically increase. Many have said that Times Square is a completely different world at night: the daytime mask of restraint is removed and the area's real face is revealed. Gone are the shoppers, the commuters, and the business people. They have made it to the safety of their homes and do not venture back. The people on the street at night are different, the danger and risks are greater, and the activity is about as "street level" as it gets anywhere in the city. There are more drug dealers, more prostitutes, and more criminal activity. The people on the street assume that if one is in this area late at night, there is a specific reason. The natives say that there are three kinds of people on the Deuce and 8th Avenue: "them that be sellin' it, them that be buyin' it, and those tryin' to bust it up."

*   *   *   *

It is Friday night, about 12:30 a.m. Friday is payday for many people and the street is alive with activity. Drugs are being sold at a steady pace, and although it is bitterly cold tonight, many people are on the street. In front of the entrance to the Hotel Carter, a few prostitutes stand, stamping their feet on the sidewalk to keep warm. No doubt they hope to "score a trick" and stay inside for the night. I am standing inside the foyer of El Sid's Electronics Emporium trying, without success, to ward off the chilling cold and the biting wind. The wind is so strong and sharp that my eyes water unless I stand with my back to it.

Three young Caucasian males who appear to be college students are making an awkward attempt to buy drugs. I surmise that they are suburban students attracted to the night life of the city. They are approached by Raffi, a Jamaican drug dealer, who convinces them his ganja, although a little more expensive than what they could get from other dealers, is of much higher quality. He says: "Ya, mon, you buy me stuff, mon, you go higher than the clouds. And you don't need that much either, mon. Buy me stuff, you see. Everybody here know me mon, you ask and dey tell you. So what you gonna do mon? You gonna buy from me or what?"

The three students leave. Raffi smiles at no one in particular, revealing extremely large, white teeth, and then laughs heartily. I have known Raffi since January, about a month. He has told me that he holds two different bags of marijuana: one is for his regular customers or people he thinks he can not fool, and the other, which is little more than a mix of herbs such as tea, oregano, ground parsley, and sometimes a dash of low-grade marijuana, is for customers like the students.

About a half hour later, I see a boy of about twelve years old walking up 42nd Street toward Broadway. He is rather small and is wearing jeans, a red sweater, and a denim jacket. Given that the temperature is 16 degrees farenheit, according to the *Newsweek* building, and the wind makes it feel even colder, I suspect that something is wrong. As he continues to walk purposefully, I see a large black man following him. He grabs the boy by the arm and pulls him close, speaking to him in what sounds like an angry tone. He points his right finger in the boy's face, emphasizing each word. The boy wrestles free and begins to walk faster than before, while the man stands on the sidewalk, yelling, "Don't you be walkin' away from me you little motherfucker, I ain't done with you yet."

The boy continues to ignore the man. He heads in my direction, and I can see that he looks worried and afraid. This kid is not wise to the ways of the streets, this is a lamb in a den of hungry wolves who have caught the scent of easy prey. As the boy makes his way up 42nd Street, other men catch sight of him. After seeing the first man throw his hands up in disgust and walk away, they conclude that the boy is fair game.

Time after time, men stop the boy on the sidewalk and try to talk to him while blocking his way. Nonetheless, the boy trudges on until he is met by a tall, thin Hispanic man who falls into step with him: a different tactic from that of his predecessors. The two are close enough to me now that I can hear the conversation. The man says: "Yo man I ain't gonna hurt you, I just want to talk to you, that's all. You wanna make money? I know you need money—everybody need money. All I'm askin' is if you want some."

The boy, who stops to ponder the offer (the nature of which I could not overhear), shakes his head. He is smart enough to continue walking after he gives his answer, but fails to realize that this man is determined to elicit his cooperation. "Look you little motherfucker," the man hisses, "If you don't go with me, I'll sharp [cut, slash or stab] your ass up right here and now. So you got a choice, you either go with me or you don't go nowhere."

At this point, the boy must have realized the extent of the danger. His eyes became wide with fear, and he looked at the man and in all directions, either seeking help or considering his escape route. He was out of his element. I had no doubt at this point that he was in serious trouble. In the span of perhaps two minutes, while going from one end of 42nd Street to the middle of the street, the boy had been accosted and threatened twice, and he had been propositioned four additional times for his services or his time.

Motivated, perhaps, by fear, anger, or desperation, the boy slammed his foot into the man's instep and took off into the street. With tires screeching and horns blaring, he made it to the other side of the street and disappeared into the night. The older man stood alone, yelling a long stream of expletives and rubbing his ankle. He eventually limped off, perhaps in search of medical treatment, sympathy, or more likely, another victim. This incident typifies how quickly things can degenerate in this area. The situation could have easily become more dangerous, and I was even contemplating what I could do to help when the boy saved himself. Many people come to Times Square in search of thrills but end up getting more excitement—and danger—than they were prepared for.

Hustlers are one of the most salient features of the Times Square scene, and an examination of this area that fails to include them is incomplete. The next chapter introduces the principal participants in this study as well as describing a number of features of the rest of this community.

REFERENCES

Bloom, Ken. 1991. *Broadway: An Encyclopedic Guide to the History, People and Places of Times Square*. New York: Facts on File.

Dunlap, David W. 1990. "A Changing Times Square: But for Now, Cleanup Agency Collects the Rent." the *New York Times*, August 12, p. R14.

Erenberg, Lewis A. 1981. *Steppin' Out*. Westport, Conn.: Greenwood Press.

Kornblum, William and Terry Williams. *West Forty-Second Street: The Bright Light Zone*. New York: Basic Books. (in press).

New York City. 1991. *Mass Transit Authority Report*. New York: Mass Transit Authority.

New York City. Office of Midtown Enforcement, *Summary of Criminal Activity on West 42nd Street: Eighth Avenue to Seventh Avenue, 1980-91*. New York: Office of Midtown Enforcement.

3

The Cast

A young man, whom I'll call Apache, stands on the corner of the
Deuce and 8th Avenue in front of the Port Authority Bus Terminal. He
is tall, standing just under six feet, and his lithe, 150 pound body is
accentuated by a green tank top and black stretch shorts. Crew socks
and Reebok "Pumps," a popular sneaker, round out his "look," and
a few thin gold chains shine brightly against his bronze skin. His hair
is jetblack, slicked back and glistens in the June sun. Numerous prison
tattoos, thin lines devoid of color or creativity, are barely discernible
because of his dark skin. They line his forearms, biceps, and upper
shoulders, serving as a reminder of his wife and son's names.

If he were to lift his shirt, the scars from a life of knife fights and
gun shots wounds would show in stark contrast to the smooth texture
of the rest of his body. To the uninformed, however, he appears to be
a clean, "smooth," and friendly youth. Today, Apache is "working
the Deuce." He is an older hustler, twenty-one years of age, but his
seven year's experience in the trade belie his youthful appearance.
Apache is a leader within the hustling community. His experience, as
well as his ability to make money through prostitution and other
ventures, earn him a great deal of respect and status. Many hustlers,
especially the young and inexperienced, often go to Apache for advice
and money. They also try to hang out with him in hopes that he will
teach them a few of the few more lucrative tricks of the trade.

Apache was one of the first hustlers I met in Times Square. An
astute observer, he quickly caught on to the nuances of field research.
A native New Yorker who now lives in Queens, he is married and has
a ten month old son. Most of his time is spent dodging his parole officer and hustling to support his family. Apache is also HIV positive.

In many ways, Apache is typical of most street hustlers in Times

Square. As Tables 3.1 and 3.2 demonstrate, whether they are young (between fourteen and seventeen years old) or older (over eighteen, with most falling into the eighteen to twenty-one age group), the vast majority are Hispanic. The term Hispanic can include Puerto Rican, Spaniard, Mexican, Dominican, or any combination. Consequently, categorization is a tricky proposition. I used a self-report measure of ethnicity and simply asked with what race or ethnicity a person identified. For instance, in the case of individuals who are both Puerto Rican and Dominican, most identify themselves as the former rather than the latter, and as a result, this is how I would classify them as well.

Two-thirds of the younger hustlers and almost three-fourths of the older hustlers in Times Square are Hispanic. Of all the hustlers I interviewed, thirty, or 86%, were Hispanic. African Americans constituted four, or 11%, of interviewees. The Caucasian population, a distinct minority in the Times Square hustling scene, was represented by a single male, constituting 3% of the total.

While I have mentioned that mine was not a scientific sample but rather a Times Square "chunk of humanity," the boys' estimation of

Table 3.1

Race and Sexual Preference of
Interviewed Times Square Hustlers under Age 18 (14-17)

	Hispanic	African Amer.	Caucasian
Heterosexual	66% (8)	——	——
Homosexual	17% (2)	100% (1)	——
Bisexual	17% (2)	——	——
Totals	100% (12)	100% (1)	——

their demographics are consistent with these figures. By their own estimation, hustling in Times Square is a distinctly Hispanic phenomenon. "Ninety percent of all the hustlers out here are Puerto Rican. Clients want a young, skinny-looking Puerto Rican, not a white boy," said Apache. "And at one time, a lotta blacks were goin' with the tricks, but it ain't that way no more. Now it's like, maybe, 10% black and the rest is Puerto Ricans that they go with."

Apache raises an interesting question concerning the reasons for the large representation of Puerto Ricans in the market as well as when this domination came about. Although no one can really explain when or why, at some point Puerto Rican hustlers indeed began to make up a substantial proportion of the hustling population. Another interesting aspect of this phenomenon is that virtually all the clients are middle to lower class Caucasians. These issues of ethnicity and social class are extremely complicated and difficult to resolve and I raise them not to offer an explanation but rather to illustrate the peculiarity of the hustling market.

Table 3.2

Race and Sexual Preference of
Interviewed Times Square Hustlers Age 18 and Over (18-35)

	Hispanic	African Amer.	Caucasian
Heterosexual	72% (13)	33% (1)	100% (1)
Homosexual	22% (4)	33% (1)	——
Bisexual	6% (1)	33% (1)	——
Totals	100% (18)	100% (3)	100% (1)

Note: Column two totals 99% due to rounding.

Traditionally, hustling has been associated with homosexuality. This is logical since most hustling activities are homosexual in nature. Most of the early, and some of the more recent, literature on the subject agrees that hustling is a homosexual phenomenon (Ginsburg 1967; Caukins and Coombs 1976; Craft 1966; Deisher, Eisner and Sulzbacher 1969). More recently Pleak and Meyer-Bahlburg (1990) argued that most of the hustlers in Manhattan are homosexual. However, while some hustlers are, in fact, gay, there are a number of studies that indicate otherwise (Allen 1980; Coombs 1974; Jersild 1956; MacNamara 1965; Reiss 1961; Weisberg 1985).

Most of the hustlers I know in Times Square, identify themselves as heterosexual. As Tables 3.1 and 3.2 demonstrate, eight of the young hustlers and fifteen of the older ones identified themselves as heterosexual. Thus, a total of twenty-three or 66% said they were straight and either had girlfriends or wives. A total of eight hustlers, or 23%, stated they were homosexual, and four, or 11%, considered themselves bisexual. This is a thorny issue which is problematic to verify. In some instances I was able to independently determine a boy's sexual identity beyond self-report, such as by asking other hustlers or visiting the home to meet his wife or live-in companion. While this test is obviously not foolproof, in these instances, all individuals had been honest in their statements.

Additionally, as Reiss (1961) and others discovered, the range of activities in which boys will engage has much to do with validating their sexual identity. Those hustlers who engaged in active fellatio or anal intercourse were more likely to admit to being gay or bisexual, whereas heterosexual hustlers would only allow passive fellatio or masturbation (either active or passive). This was also the case with the boys in Times Square.

Most of the homosexual hustlers in New York City work in the Greenwich Village section of the city, notably Christopher Street as well as the piers of the West Side Highway. Others frequent Midtown Manhattan, near 53rd Street between First and Second Avenues. Heterosexual hustlers, on the other hand, seem to confine themselves to the Times Square section, mostly on 42nd Street and 8th Avenue. This is not to say that these are exclusive boundaries, but as a general rule, they serve as an adequate marker. I have met homosexual hustlers in the Port Authority Bus Terminal and heterosexual hustlers in the Village, but it seems that most travel in their own exclusive circles.

Raul is another example of a heterosexual hustler. He is bigger and taller than average: about 6'2'' and approximately 215 pounds. Usually clad in jeans, tan workboots, a tee shirt, and a Cleveland Indians baseball cap, he is an imposing figure. Two days a week he works out at the Times Square Gym, a boxing club of considerable renown. He is nearly twenty-eight and has been hustling since he was age seventeen. He lives in the Bronx and, like Apache, is on public assistance. For Raul, hustling provides a tax-free way to supplement his income and support his drug habit. The income from prostitution serves as his spending money.

Raul's standing in the community is based on his fearlessness and reputation for violence. Few have ever walked away victorious from a confrontation with him. A fighter who likes the physical contact, he serves as protector for a number of hustlers in the area, a role he learned to play in prison. As he explained:

> I was in for armed robbery in Clinton, you know upstate. So one day this guy, this little shit of a guy comes up to me and says Oak is after him. Now Oak is a badass nigger who looks like a fuckin' oak tree. This little guy, I can't even remember his name now, he tells me he'll pay me whatever I want if I could take care of him, you know. So I did, I went to Oak and we got busy, you know. It was the worst fight of my life, but I walked away. No problem. Well, after that it was easy. When I got out and started hangin' around here, I found out lots of guys get into some shit with somebody and they need help. Just like prison. So I help them out, you know, for the right price.

Raul is admired, feared, and respected in the community not only because of his fighting skills, but also due to his sense of fair play. I found that at times he prefers to settle a dispute amicably rather than resort to violence as a first response. However, if the diplomatic approach fails, Raul's quick hands are often the deciding factor.

While Raul's reputation as an enforcer accords him status, it sometimes interferes with his hustling opportunities. Many tricks avoid him, feeling intimidated by his aggressive style. On the other hand, a number of clients actually prefer this type of encounter and are willing to take the risk. Thus, although Raul has fewer clients, almost all are ''steadies.'' Coupled with the money he makes by protecting others, Raul says he earns about two hundred dollars a week. Lately, however,

Raul has begun to drift back into the use of heroin, a habit he says he
had kicked when he was in his early twenties. Until recently, marijuana
was his drug of choice and he avoided crack and other hard drugs
because of their detrimental effects. He said:

> Man I saw enough of that shit [crack] to make me want to
> stay away from it forever. I tried it and I tried snortin'
> cocaine, I just did not like it. When I was doin' drugs, I
> only did dope [heroin], but that fucked me up too, so now
> I'll drink my beer and smoke my pot, but that's about all I
> can do.

His slippage back into a steady diet of heroin, as we shall see, lead to
a number of problems for Raul.

Flacco has just turned thirty years old, has been hustling since he
was age fifteen, and is one of the oldest hustlers I have met. Like
Apache and Raul, Flacco is highly respected. In his case, however, this
standing in the social hierarchy is based on time spent in the trade.
Much in the same way that older workers are highly respected for their
wisdom and experience, younger hustlers seek him out for his advice
and wisdom.

He has turned tricks, danced in the clubs, "worked sugar daddies"
for money, clothes, and housing and finally developed such an extensive and elaborate network of friends, colleagues and associates that he
rarely needs to hustle any longer and likes to think of himself as semi-
retired. Part of this designation has to do with the fact that Flacco is
bisexual. He no longer has to hustle since there are older gay men who
will take care of him. At the same time, he has numerous female
companions with whom he stays from time to time.

Humphreys (1970) described what he calls the "aging out" process.
With regard to hustling, as the young men begin to look older, they
become less desirable. As a result, boys usually find fewer
opportunities to earn money through prostitution and must find some
other money-making venture. Flacco is just beginning to experience the
process, but he says he no longer needs to turn tricks. He still has a
small number of steady clients, mostly older gay men who have grown
fond of him. As he told me:

> I look at it this way. I don't have to hustle any more. I
> don't have to worry about paying rent or buying food or

any of that stuff. And I don't have to worry about somebody finding me if I don't want to be found. I have a few guys I stay with regularly, you know, some nights I stay with this guy, and then a few nights later I stay with another guy. I do this all week long. I get fed real good, they take care of me, and they give me money to spend. I got my pot, I got some money for a movie if I want, I'm all set. I got some money saved up in case something happens to me, and if I get really fucked up or something, I can always find a job for a little while. See that's the thing. I don't need to hustle. I'm past all that. Now I go there because my friends are there. I can go, hang out, bullshit, maybe play a little ball if I want; it's easy, it's real easy. And I been there so long that now people come to me for advice; yeah, I'm like the fuckin' godfather. You can't beat that, man. I mean people come to *me* and ask me what to do.

Flacco's position in the culture is that of an elder who, although essentially out of the day-to-day action, remains on the scene for the social advantages: he gets to hang out with his friends. There is also the added advantage to remaining in the trade—he offers his wisdom to others and gains status by providing it.

These three individuals, representing different but important roles in the hustling culture, were integral in establishing my own role within the community. While time does not permit me to describe each hustler I encountered, a few others deserve mention. Collectively, these portraits represent some of the most salient features of the hustling life-style, as well as some of the difficulties of managing it.

Pretty Boy Tony is a young African American, seventeen years old, who spends most of his days either in the Port Authority Bus Terminal or in front of one of the peep shows on 8th Avenue. His short hair is accentuated with a three-inch razor line which starts on the left side of his head and curves along his scalp. He has a very high opinion of himself, which is reflected in his wardrobe. He says his mood dictates his outfit for the day:

Well, like, some days I get up, I'm stayin' with my aunt in Brooklyn you know. She don't like me goin' out and stuff, but she can't stop me. She think I be runnin' with a gang or somethin.' Anyway, I get up in the mornin' and if I feel like lookin' pretty, then I might wear some nice clothes and gold, lots a gold, cause the tricks, they like a pretty looking black boy standin' around smilin' at them and shit. But other days, like today, maybe I don't care. I dress like I like. Jeans, my Nikes, and a raggedy tee shirt. I ain't got nothin' to prove to nobody! If a trick don't like what he see, he can go and find somebody else. [Pause.] But like in the summer time and shit? When it be real hot? I be out there in my tight stretch pants or maybe. [Pause.] I got this jumpsuit I wear. It's like a tank top and a pair of short shorts, but they all one piece, you know what I'm sayin? And it's yellow, so the men know what I got under the hood and they know they can find me too. But it's just like anybody else, some days I wanna look good and other days I don't give a shit.

Pretty Boy Tony is usually clean and he tends to smell of cocoa butter, but when he smiles, large gaps show between his teeth. Many are crooked and discolored, which forces his jawline off center. The clothes he wears are never as lavish as he would like people to believe. Tony perceives himself as irresistible to men and women alike. As he states, he has nothing to prove. He can dress almost like a bum and men will still find him attractive. In some ways, this allows him, he thinks, to be selective in his choice of clients.

Although uncertain of his sexual identity, Tony is leaning toward homosexuality and states he is currently trying to make up his mind which way he would like to "swing." He claims that bisexuality, or "playing for both teams" does not interest him since he believes people should be decisive about who they are and what they want. Bisexuals, in his estimation, can not make up their minds and remain completely undecided. Tony turns three to four tricks almost every day. Although he began hustling only last year, his inexperience is overcome by his work ethic.

During the day, Tony stands in one of several regular spots like a soldier on post, waiting for a trick to happen by. When he is finished with a client, he returns to the general area and begins a new vigil. He knows few people in Times Square, perhaps because he keeps to himself and is focused on making money. I get the sense that Tony has a goal outside hustling. He does not socialize with many other hustlers. He characterizes his position in Times Square in this way:

> Well, I know a lot of people and they know me. I mean, I'm here every damn day, but I don't hang out with them. I don't want to get too tight with them cause that can only get me in trouble. I don't want no trouble, I don't want nobody. I say hi to lots of people, but that don't mean I wanna hang out with them, you know?

Maintaining a social distance between himself and other hustlers in some ways makes Tony think he is above street life, although he spends more time in the street than most of the others. He is a workhorse, but this does not seem to accord him any status, nor does it seem to bother him that he is becoming more like his colleagues every day. He is a prima donna who, despite his air of superiority, is more involved in "the life" than he realizes or cares to admit. I also believe that Tony gets a greater reward from hustling than just the monetary remuneration, but he has not reached the same conclusion.

Canno is the reformist within the group. A Dominican/Puerto Rican mix, he is twenty-one years old and has only recently been released from prison. He has been a drug dealer, an armed robber, and an accomplice to murder. He is also one of the few hustlers with any type of relationship with his family of origin. He maintains ties with his father, although they are quite fragile. His father works as an auto mechanic, but before that he spent fifteen years in prison on a manslaughter charge: a night of drinking led to an argument with an acquaintance over money, a knife was pulled, and the ensuing brawl left one man dead and Canno's father in prison.

Canno himself spent four years in prison for selling drugs and the attempted murder of a police officer. The latter charge is false according to Canno since all he did was point his weapon at an undercover officer, who had not identified himself. Nonetheless, the entire incident and two others like it have had a sweeping impact on Canno's life and led to several dramatic changes in his life-style.

Canno and his brother robbed a number of drug corners. They would steal money and drugs from the dealers and then take over the sales operation. They were eventually caught and sentenced, but not before Canno's brother raped the fifteen-year-old daughter of a Colombian drug dealer. Canno stated:

Yeah, what happened was, me and my brother, I'm the oldest. We were only a year apart. Uh, of course, I was the black sheep of the family and my brother just, like, followed in my footsteps. By the time he really got into the business I was already dealing drugs and doin' armed robberies. My specialty was knockin' off other drug spots. See the reason why we did that was as long as we [Pause] once you stick them up, and we get a mound of drugs and money, then they figure they can't go back there cause we gonna keep robbin' them. So they leave that spot. And then we put our drugs in there. But that's what we did and we started growing and growing. Then my brother came into the business, his initiation was to do this job with me. The job we did was to knock off a Colombian drug spot. When we did this, my brother raped a Colombian girl, which happened to be a supplier's daughter.

So in the first place, Colombians don't take no shit, and especially something like that. So now they were lookin' for us. And they found us. See, once they found out where my brother was, they knew where I was. See, I was the crazy one. So they figured, if my brother's in jail, then I gotta be too. And it took them almost a month and a half to find me. And man, did they find me. That's why I say I was lucky, cause they was supposed to beat me physically and I was supposed to be left for dead. I got out of that, and when I came home in September of last year, the first thing me and my father do is to go over there and deal with them. And I told my father, ''I don't think we should go,'' but he said: ''no no no, if they gonna kill you, they gonna kill you one way or the other, so you might as well go out like a trooper and go to their fucking place. The only thing that can happen is we talk it out and then clear the air.''

And when we got over there, the first thing the Colombian said was, ''I'm sorry what happened to you. Your brother—I don't give a fuck, he had it coming to him. I found out you had nothing to do with it. All you was doin' was stickin' up the spot. The money and the drugs I don't give a fuck about, but my daughter got hurt. And we was really lookin' for your brother. Once we knocked off your brother, and then they got to you, I got the word and told them to stop, don't even continue the process." And, see, the daughter was there, the daughter was in the apartment at the time me and my father were there. And I looked at her, and she said "You was trying to tell him [your brother] that's not why we were there." And it's true, I tried to tell my brother. We had everybody tied up. It was, like, $84,000 in drugs alone. In cocaine alone on the table. And there was two suitcases with at least $35,000 in cash.

So when I turned around, I picked up that last briefcase, and I turned around and looked, my brother ain't there. So then I hear muffled noises in the bedroom. I open the door and here he was, like, rapin' this girl. I'm, like, "Yo what the fuck are you doin'! Let's go, man. We not here for that. That's wrong man." And he's, like, "It's only gonna take five minutes hold up." And he's goin' at her. And I'm, like, "Yo man, that's fucked up. I'm grabbin' the shit man, I'm goin' man. I'm leavin' you behind, you know." And he said, "Okay." So I turned around and grabbed the suitcases, grabbed the drugs, put them in the suitcases and when I opened up the door he was there, he was, like, zippin' up his pants. See, and the thing is, that Colombian girl had to tell her father the truth. She told him, "yeah he's the guy that came in here and tied everybody up and stole the money and the drugs, but that's all he did." And that's true! I bust in there and told them, "nothin' moves but the money." And they were cool about it, they knew. I mean I wasn't gonna do no ass busting, cause I know one day it could happen to me. But my brother had to do it, and they killed him the day after Christmas 1990, and they got to me on January 11th.

Although seriously injured, with a severed nerve in his leg, a broken arm, nose, and three ribs, and various razor cuts resulting in nearly sixty stitches, Canno survived. However, this near-death experience changed his outlook on life. Another brush with death at the hands of a different inmate who was armed with a knife led to a second stay in the hospital. It was at this point that Canno swore off drug dealing, and using drugs, as well as all other types of criminal activity.

Throwing himself into as many training programs and church-related activities as he could manage, Canno was determined to reform himself. Upon release from prison, he took three part-time jobs. One was as a bouncer in a bar in the Bronx. He stated:

> I started working in a bar as a waiter and a bouncer. That's how I got this (points to a three-inch scar behind left ear). [It looks like either a razor cut or a bottle] Yeah, you right, it was a razor cut. One of the customers was gettin' obnoxious. So I pulled him outside, I told him, "Either you calm down or you leave the premises." He pushes his body up against mine and said, "What the fuck you gonna do?" So I punched him in the mouth and let him know that I am the bouncer. I'm the man here! So right away he puts his fists up, "Let's fight!" So I didn't see him spit out no razor, like in the institution, we spit out razors. I can carry a razor in my mouth all fuckin' day and it don't bother me. So I didn't see him spit out no razor, I look at his hands, I didn't see nothin'. So I'm gettin' ready to fight, you know.
>
> He goes and swings, and usually when someone swings toward your face they go towards your jaw. So I saw a fist comin', and I turned like this, and the next thing you know, a razor hits me in the neck. He had it right between his fingers. So when I turned around, I could feel the blood on my neck. I felt my neck and said, "oh shit." The next thing I know, I grab my jacket cause I had money in my jacket, ran outside, jumped into a cab and went to the hospital. Twenty-two stitches: eight inside, fourteen outside. The doctor said he cut a small artery, but he said it was an inch and a half from my jugular vein. He said "you very lucky." I said to myself, what does it take? I almost get killed in the institution, and now an inch and a half from my jugular vein, twenty two stitches. I lived through that. I said, man, if a cat got nine lives, a human can't have more than three. That's like one of the other things that got me really calmed down.

At this point, Canno decided to stay out of all types of trouble. He joined self-help groups, volunteered for Meals on Wheels, helped out at Narcotics Anonymous (NA) and Alcoholics Anonymous (AA) meetings, and became an AIDS volunteer for a local outreach program. Unfortunately, these socially conscious efforts did not pay the rent. He lost his jobs as a bouncer and waiter when he was injured in the bar fight, but he continues to work as a grocery store clerk three days a week. While keeping his promise to stay away from a life of crime, he returned to hustling to cover his living expenses. Now every day he hustles for twenty dollars and then goes home. He knows many people in the area and considers them his friends, but he says he knows that if he hangs out with them, it will eventually get him in trouble. Instead, he talks to many of the young hustlers about the trade. He tries to get them to wear condoms and to stay away from overnight tricks or those that want to take the boys home. "That's where it'll happen. If they gonna hurt you, they'll do it there," he says. He tries to get hustlers to seek treatment if they have a drug habit. He chides the ones he thinks are HIV positive to be tested and talk to counselors at the Association for Drug Abuse Prevention and Treatment (ADAPT) or one of the local outreach programs. He also tries to help the hustlers that have no place to stay.

Because of Canno's previous standing in the community, where he was regarded as a "bad-ass," he can get away with some of this preaching. Some hustlers listen to him and take his advice, although recently there have been grumbled epithets of "preacher" and "social worker" made in reference to him. He lives in an old, inexpensive hotel nearby. The manager is a friend of his father and gives him a discount on the room. Canno goes out every day looking for tricks, and at the same time, trying to save a few lives.

Mad Max is a crackhead. He is eighteen but looks like he is in his late thirties. His dark, wavy hair has been pulled back into a crude, short ponytail. His attempt to grow a beard does little to improve his overall physical appearance: his facial hair is insufficient to make a full beard. It is easy to see that his eclectic wardrobe is based on what was available at Covenant House or Streetworks Project, where he often goes for clothes and food. Dark circles form half-moons under his eyes and his sallow cheeks give him a depressed and defeated look. His face is lined with fatigue and the aging process hastened by crack and other drugs.

Mad Max is homeless. He is a Puerto Rican whose mother lives on the island. He calls about twice a week and asks her to send him money, but she rarely does so. He sleeps in the bus terminal, Grand Central Station, Penn Station, tricks' houses, or wherever he can. He spent time at Covenant House but left because of what he calls the "strictness of the place." He refused to abide by the rules and was promptly asked to leave.

Max spends all the money he earns on crack. I learned most about the crack trade from observing Mad Max, accompanying him and a few associates while copping the drug, or playing lookout while they smoked it. Max also smokes marijuana and has tried heroin, but he prefers crack. One of the most remarkable things about Mad Max is that despite the debilitating effects of crack, he is quite observant and knowledgeable. He is also very good at acting "straight," even when high. In fact, he is so adept at this ploy that he convinced a local Colombian gang to allow him to sell crack on one of their corners. They pay him ten dollars for every bundle (ten bags) of heroin he sells and a percentage of what he brings in from selling crack vials.

Mad Max is a very intelligent and perceptive young man. He talks often about going to college someday and thinks he might want to be a mechanical engineer. He continually asked me when I would have a chapter of this volume ready for him to read. He spends almost every day hustling, copping, hanging out, or trying to find ways to buy more drugs. He has a criminal record, but for most of these crimes he was considered a youthful offender. As a result, he has spent less time incarcerated for his offenses than had he been convicted as an adult. Mad Max considers himself a heterosexual and looks on his hustling skills much in the same way as a majority of hustlers.

Eddie is a 6'4" 160 pound Puerto Rican hustler. He is sixteen years old and HIV positive. He is still very active sexually and considers himself a bisexual who turned to men after having considerable success with females. He described the change:

> When I came out, I came all the way out. I mean, when I decided to do it, I used to wear the spike heels, the dress, the wig: the whole bit. I would put on makeup. I used to go with my friends and beat the shit outta the faggots—now I sleep with them. I go to bars and we talk about everybody, puttin' them down and shit. I just got tired of the girl thing. I mean, I had more pussy than I could ask for, them Puerto Rican girls at my school. But once I got a dick, I knew I wouldn't go back all the way. Now I go with these gay guys, they pay me to let them blow me or I blow them, it depends. And every once in a while, I'll see a girl I want and it's chill. But I got my own place, my own apartment

with my brother. He's a hustler too, but he's got some Queen [drag queen] he keeps on 34th Street, so I don't see him much.

The reason Eddie can afford his own apartment is due to his Social Security Disability benefits or as they are known on the streets, Title 19. He has qualified as being disabled and receives approximately five hundred dollars a month. Eddie knows many of the hustlers from his neighborhood in Queens as well as from the bus terminal, where he spends most of his time.

Eddie is considered the jokester or "wiseass" of the community. His voice can often be heard above the crowds outside the terminal, playfully yelling at someone or mockingly insulting the vendors or passersby. He knows almost all the uniformed police officers and banters with them at times. In response to his sarcasm, the officers frequently eject him from the building. Typically, standing with hands on hips and donning a coy expression, Eddie will respond: "Why you always throw me out? You must like me, that's why you always lookin' for me. You know, you and me, we could do some serious things together, lovely, lovely boy!" This leaves Eddie squealing with laughter.

Eddie refers to himself as a "goody-goody" because he avoids fights and other types of trouble. His biggest offense is that he sometimes gets arrested for prostitution. He spends most of his time at the terminal, drawn like others, by the interactions and the hustling opportunities. Eddie's standing in the community is assured. He is looked after and protected, especially by Raul, who said:

> It is hard not to like Eddie. It is impossible to stay mad at him—he is just one of those people who, while pissing you off, cracks you up at the same time. Yeah, he is a pain in the ass sometimes, but just when you think you've had enough, he goes and does something nice for you or he'll make you laugh when you really need it.

Among all the people I met during the course of this project, Eddie's image will remain vivid because he is somewhat of an anomaly. He genuinely likes people, and they him, but at the same time, he remains sexually active even though he is infected with the HIV virus. He is careful to use condoms but only with his regular partners. In fact he is the only hustler I know who keeps a constant supply on him. However, while his humor and colorful persona make people smile and laugh, there is a dark side to Eddie that must be taken into account. As his story unfolded, especially as it relates to his attitudes about AIDS and hustling, this became increasingly apparent.

Dead Head is the only Caucasian hustler I have met. Twenty-one years old, a devout Grateful Dead fan (as if there are any other kind), and a full blooded Irishman complete with a healthy collection of freckles and reddish hair, Dead Head is homeless and came to Times Square and hustling in a mostly traditional manner, but with a few unusual twists. He said:

> Well, I had traveled with the Dead: they came to Florida. I traveled with them up to Atlanta. And I traveled over here to Suffolk County, all right? Pennsylvania, the whole bit. I came here at the Garden. And while I was at the Garden, and while I was here I lost my friend and I couldn't get a ride out. [So they don't know where you are?] Right! So I'm gonna have to wait till September again to find them. [Why?] Because the Dead comes back to the Garden in September, and I know they'll be there and I know their van. [When was this, when did you lose your friends?] September!
>
> [Where are you staying?] Nowhere! [So where are you sleeping, in the terminal here?] Naw they kick you outta the terminal. One o'clock in the morning, the terminal closes until 6 a.m. So they kick you out. So right now, I have a spot where I sleep. Over on 7th Avenue in the Fashion Building, where they got the statue of the man sewing? Well, the indentation there? I sleep there at night. [Is that where all your stuff is?] Actually, what I got as far as clothing is concerned is clothes on my back. But I got hooked up with Streetworks Project. They give me a change of clothing or showers.
>
> [Pause] It's like out here on the street, and it's really fucked up. So, um, then I started hangin' out here and old men would come over to you and they wanna take you into the peep shows and maybe they wanna blow you or maybe you have to blow them or whatever, and it's great money. And, I mean, a lotta hustlers like me, we don't really want

to do it, but we need to do it to get by because there are no jobs, really, in the city. Put in your book, man, not every hustler does it by choice. We don't do it by choice. It's, like, to survive. See, I can't get a job cause I can't get a residence. I gotta have an address or I can't get a job. And they'll check, too. What they do is they want a phone number that they can call you and reach you at. See, you put an application in and they'll say, we'll call you within a couple of days, and they won't even talk to you unless you have a phone. So I can't get a job.

In some ways, Dead Head is typical of many of the hustlers in Times Square, and in other ways he does not quite fit. For instance, like other hustlers, Dead Head lacks any type of family structure. In fact, he has no living relatives. Like some hustlers, he is without financial resources and has turned to hustling as a form of survival. However, Dead Head is an unusually compassionate member of this community.

Always lending a sympathetic ear or the last puff of his only cigarette, Dead Head tries to make the most of a rather bleak situation. I have seen many instances where he could have easily stolen a suitcase or a purse left in a telephone cubicle, but instead, he has scolded the passenger for their negligence. Additionally, Dead Head avoids hard drugs, preferring marijuana and large quantities of beer. While this may relate to his financial straits, crack vials can also be purchased for as little as three dollars in Times Square, but he simply stays away from them.

These are a few of the characters I have met along the way. They represent some of the contrasts and key components in the culture. While I will use the dialogue and comments of others in the coming pages, this is the "cast of recognition." Moreover, while I obtained related information from a host of hustlers, I will draw more heavily from those with whom I spent the most time. What is it like to be a hustler? What goes on? How does the transaction generally take place? These and other questions will be addressed in the next chapter, where I outline a typical day in the life of a hustler.

REFERENCES

Allen, Donald. 1980. "Male Prostitutes: A Psychosocial Study." *Archives of Sexual Behavior* 9(5):399-426.

Caukins, Sivan E., and Neil R. Coombs. 1976. "The Psychodynamics of Male Prostitution." *American Journal of Psychotherapy* 30:441-451.

Coombs, Neil. 1974. "Male Prostitution: A Psychological View of Behavior." *American Journal of Orthopsychiatry* 44:782-789.

Craft, Michael. 1966. "Boy Prostitutes and Their Fate." *British Journal of Psychiatry* 112:1111-1114.

Deisher, Robert W., Victor Eisner, and Stephen I. Sulzbacher. 1969. "The Young Male Prostitute." *Pediatrics* 43(6):936-941.

Ginsburg, Kenneth N. 1967. "The Meat-Rack: A Study of the Male Homosexual Prostitute." *American Journal of Psychotherapy* 21(2):170-185.

Humphreys, Laud. 1970. *Tearoom Trade: Impersonal Sex in Public Places.* London: Duckworth.

Jersild, Jens. 1956. *Boy Prostitution.* Copenhagen, Denmark: C. E. Gad.

MacNamara, Donal E. J. 1965. "Male Prostitution in American Cities: A Socioeconomic or Pathological Phenomenon?" *American Journal of Orthopsychiatry* 35:204.

Pleak, Richard R., and Heino Meyer-Bahlburg. 1990. "Sexual Behavior and AIDS Knowledge of Young Male Prostitutes in Manhattan." *Journal of Sex Research* 27(4):557-587.

Reiss, Albert J., Jr. 1961. "The Social Integration of Queers and Peers." *Social Problems* 9(2):102-20.

Weisberg, Kelly D. 1985. *Children of the Night.* South Hadley, Mass.: Lexington Books.

4

A Day in the Life

A typical day for a hustler begins early, often as early as 7 a.m., and ends as late as 2 or 3 the next morning. The weekend schedule is different, beginning and ending later and sometimes involving overnight stays with clients. The excitement of the weekend contrasts with the idleness of the remaining days of the week. This chapter begins with a discussion of the trade and proceeds to the events and situations a hustler usually encounters.

THE GAME AND HOW IT IS PLAYED

The Port Authority Bus Terminal is a special place for many hustlers. Much of the hustling in Times Square occurs either in the terminal or in the peep shows. Both offer anonymity for the client because of the amount of human traffic through both places. For example, the exodus of commuters from the City, especially at rush hour, offers clients the opportunity to lose themselves in the throng of people making their way home and to carry out transactions with hustlers without attracting much attention.

One particular area in the terminal is known among hustlers and clients as the "Meat Rack." This is an area near some of the departure gates where the majority of hustling takes place. When the two parties reach an agreement, they go to a variety of places: the peep shows, a local hotel, the client's apartment or car, or one of the restrooms inside the terminal. However, the latter are now considered less satisfactory as a sanctuary for hustlers as a result of a new aggressive police presence, which includes undercover operations. These areas are now used sparingly or for limited activities, such as what Lite described:

I don't do nothin' that I [Pause], I don't do nothin' [Pause], the farthest thing I did was to jerk another man off, you know what I'm saying? But I never sucked a dick, never fucked another person. I tell them straight up, you know, like they say: "Yo you wanna come with me? You know, I'll give you $70." But then when we start walkin', I'll say, "Stop," and "What you all about man? What you want me to do?" I'll say, "Listen, I don't get fucked and I don't fuck nobody." The only thing I do is jerk off and I will let them watch. I'll strip for them too and let them look at my body.

But no kissing, I don't kiss no men. Sometimes you can catch the tricks early in the morning, too. Like I had this trick at 9 o'clock in the morning. You can catch them before they go to work or sometimes a trick will get them when they goin' into the bathroom. That's another kind of trick. You only get five dollars for the bathroom. You go to the bathroom and make like you peein' and somebody's watchin' the door. You get it hard and then you jerk off and then they get off, but you don't do nothin', though. You don't want to come, you definitely don't want to come. Cause then you can't make no more money. If you gonna come, it's gotta be a real expensive trick or the last one you gonna do that day, and even then you charge him extra for that.

As Lite mentioned, hustling activities are marked by their diversity. A group of hustlers explained further:

Smokealot: It depends on who the trick is and what they want you to do. Like some guys will just come up to you and say how much? Right then you know they be Five-0 [the police] because they got to get you to admit the price first. But some of the tricks will come up to you and ask you what your name is, what you like to do, if you wanna get high or somethin' like that. We work out an arrangement depending on what the trick wants. I only go with tricks I know so I ain't gonna get picked up [arrested]. But other guys will pick up anybody. And usually, depending on what they want, you can make anywhere from 30 to 40 dollars a trick. See, it depends on a lotta factors like what they want, how long they wanna go. It's just like females, you know what I'm sayin? But, like, for an average, it's about 30 dollars. But you always gotta be clockin' [observing or watching closely] the man to make sure he ain't Five-0.

Canno: Well, a lot of it depends on how long it takes them to come. Also, you gotta know what kind of things that get them off. So you gotta have the knack. Sometimes they get off by watching you come. I mean, I have a trick that wants me to come in, take my clothes off and pose for him, flexin' and shit, you know. Sometimes there are people that can't come, you gotta make 'em come, that's your job. Then there's overnights. I tell them straight up. Fifty dollars alone for me just to go to your house. Then there's another $50 to do anything, and another $50 to stay over. So it's like a hundred and fifty dollars. And, like, different guys work out different arrangements. Like this one john, he'll take a twenty dollar bill and rip it in half. He'll give you half and take half. So if he feels he's satisfied, he'll give you the other half and you just tape it and spend it. But if he's not happy, we both lose.

Raul: A lotta the hustling that goes on here ain't all that bad. I mean you go with a guy, maybe he's a member of the nickel and dime club. Those are the guys who pay you five or ten dollars and they blow you or jerk you off. We call them the nickel and dime club cause they be a lot of lonely old gay guys who are on welfare that come here and pick up guys. It takes maybe ten minutes. Sometimes they get off just watchin' you take off your clothes. Or they suck on your knob for a little bit and then they go.

But there's a lotta crazy mother-fuckers out there too, though. Like guys who will pay you good money, but the shit they want you to do is crazy, man. So it depends. Okay, I met this guy. Another guy introduced me to him. He says: "Yo you into bondage?" "Yeah I could get into it." He says: "Come on then." We got into this taxi, the guy was in the middle. He said: "Go and buy a carton of cigarettes.'' I said: ''A carton of cigarettes? I only want a pack.'' He says: ''No, not for you, I want you to burn me.'' He paid me a hundred dollars an hour to burn him with a pack of cigarettes every hour. I burned him all over his chest, his back, his legs, everywhere. At first I felt like throwin' up. I felt, like, weird, that was the first time I did that, puttin' the cigarette on him. I burned almost the whole carton on him. He paid me five hundred dollars for that.

I seen this other guy, he took me to his house. You know them things that you see on TV, they torture people, they put they head in things. [Like a pillory?] Yeah, yeah, a pillory, yeah. And he had a big old paddle, man, with spikes in it. You know what I'm talkin' about, the kind you got in schools? And he wanted me to beat him with it on his butt. I kept beating him and beating him, and I asked him is it enough and he says: ''No no I'll tell you when to stop.'' Some weird shit, man.

It appears, then, that hustling can consist of simple voyeurism, posing nude, masturbating clients, or sadomasochism, in addition to oral and anal sex.

The frequency with which the boys hustle also varies considerably. Some hustle every day, turning as many tricks as possible, while others are satisfied with one or two per day. The deciding factor, obviously, is how much money the boy needs to make. Those with drug habits, especially those addicted to crack, need to hustle as much as possible. Family men need a steady income, but since their income will be supplemented by public relief, they usually hustle less frequently than other hustlers.

Lite: I hustle at least once a day. The most people I picked up in a day? Seven. I usually pick up, like, three or four. And if I get, like, thirty dollars each time then I chill for the rest of the day. Maybe I don't come back here for two or three days.

Apache: I come down here a good four times a week, and most of the time I'll pull in two tricks a day. I could pull more, but I'll just pull two tricks. The average hustler around here? He'll pull, I guess, five to seven tricks and make himself a good three, four hundred dollars in, like, five hours.

Dead Head: Like, I gotta go with as many guys as I can cause I ain't got no money and no place to stay. Some days I'll do good and get four or five, which is maybe, like, a hundred and fifty bucks. That's cool cause then I can eat and stuff and maybe go to a movie, buy some pot or whatever. But I gotta do more than most of these guys cause I'm broke. [What is your average number for a day?] The average? Well, I guess it's probably, like, two a day. Yeah, probably one or two a day. But some days, just like anybody, I get skunked and nobody comes around.

Obviously, the amount per trick varies according to what the client requires, but the amount can also be determined by the talents of individual hustlers. For instance, some hustlers, such as Apache, are better negotiators and often convince clients to pay more than the usual fee.

While the terminal is popular, the other primary location for hustling are the peep shows. In the basement of many of these shops there is a section that caters to the homosexual client. Virtually every shop has a sign prohibiting hustling, prostitution, drug dealing, and the entry of minors, but one can easily find young men of questionable maturity standing in the long hallways.

The typical transaction in a peep show involves the hustler entering first and meeting the client near the booths. The client will have already given the boy a few quarters which gives him a legitimate reason for being there: to watch the movies. This is known among the hustlers as "going for the coins." Each party enters the booth separately, whereby the "coins," or quarters, are then put into the video machine while the sexual acts take place.

The managers and clerks of these shops are adamant about not allowing hustlers in their stores. Zenith, a clerk in one of the more popular peep shows, described it in this way:

These kids come in here lookin' to hustle and shit. They come in here and they get a boot out the other way. They ain't supposed to be here and they don't stay. They got to be 21 and then they can't hustle even if they are over 21. I ain't gonna deal with none of that shit as long as I'm the guy who makes those decisions, and I do. [How long have you worked here?] Me? I been here goin' on twelve years now. Look, there's a sign on the door that says we don't want no prostitutes, no drug dealers, no boosters [shoplifters], none of that shit. Keep it outside these walls. And to make sure none of them little assholes slide in here, I got a guy who stands in that hallway back there and throws people out if they stand there too long. We ain't got none of that in here. Maybe in the other places you do, but not here.

As we are talking, several boys who appear far younger than twenty-one walk in and begin to stroll around the store. Moreover, the hustlers tell me that it is quite easy to operate in these shops: they simply bribe the clerk and the security officer. As long as the hustler is discreet and causes no trouble, the employees are willing to ignore illicit activity. Raul tells me of his experiences with the peep shows:

See, a lotta these places will let you in the booths and shit, and sometimes there'll be more than one in a booth and that's how it goes, but they ain't supposed to let you in there with them. [Do they have guards or someone standing there?] Most of the guys they got working there are on parole and this is their job. And if they catch you, like, across the street and shit, they beat the shit outta you and take whatever money you got on you. But that don't keep 'em from takin' your money for workin' in there.

As we stand near one of the booths, a large black man who is obviously in charge bellows in a callous, gravel voice to everyone in the hallway: "Move around over here. Spend some money or get the *fuck outta here*! I don't need any of you tired-ass motherfuckers walkin' around. And the booth ain't no *fuckin' bathroom*! You wanna piss, use the *fuckin' bathroom motherfuckers*!" A few minutes later this same man catches a hustler in a booth with a trick. He is almost polite when he asks the pair to leave: "All right, fellas, that's the last time you here today, go on, get out and don't let me see your ass here. I catch you in here, you know what's gonna happen to you, right? Well then, you better not let me see you.'' Raul comments:

> You know what? They be back. You know he lets them go
> in the booth, but you gotta do him a courtesy, you know.
> It's about five dollars. If you try to go in there on your
> own, then they get tossed out. And what's five bucks from
> a hundred dollars? People want to be greedy all the time
> and keep all the money for themselves. It don't work that
> way. You be respectful and offer the man some money, he
> let you work here. And then if you fuck up, he gotta toss
> you. But if you don't, everybody's happy.

Thus, the peep shows have been, and continue to be, an integral part of the hustler's life. They offer a relatively safe working environment as well as a steady source of income. An added allure of the peep shows is that the shops also sell homosexual porno tapes. According to Apache, a number of boys have participated in the filming of these movies, and it is not uncommon to see posters advertising one of their movies on the walls of the shops. Apache and I discuss this venture:

> *MC*: I hear a lot about the movies and stuff—do you know
> anything about it? What's the deal?

> *Apache*: You talkin' about Richie. Richie, he's the one who
> makes movies, but he makes sex movies. Sex movies. He's
> alright, he's cool people.

> *MC*: How does that work?

> *Apache*: He'll come down here, and if he sees somebody
> that he likes, somebody who looks good and stuff, he'll ask
> them if they want to make a few bucks. If they do, he'll tell
> them what to do and stuff like that. And he gets them
> [Pause], the most he'll pay is like, $200 the most. So that
> ain't so good and shit. A lotta these guys around here will
> bullshit and say they got, like, $2,000 or $20,000 to do a
> movie. That's bull-shit. I know, I did it, and I seen other
> guys who did it and all they get is, like, $200.

MC: And how long does it take to make one of these movies?

Apache: It could take, like, two hours, and then he turns around and sells them to the video stores. And he sells them for forty or fifty bucks. I made, what, two, three movies.

MC: That's a good $600.

Apache: No, but I mean, for me, for me he pays more, cause I charge him extra for pictures and stuff.

MC: So he takes pictures too, for layouts and stuff in addition to the movie?

Apache: Yeah, yeah. But those kids around here, they don't know nothin' about pictures and shit, so they'll just do the movie and take pictures and shit for two hundred dollars. In the mean time, when they take pictures and do the movie with me, they pay a good three hundred, three fifty.

MC: So he's paying you for both. You don't get a percentage or anything like that, right? You just get a flat fee and he makes whatever he can off it?

Apache: You get paid for the movie, but that's about it.

MC: This may sound like a weird question but, with these movies, is there any safe sex involved?

Apache: Yeah, I just thought about safe sex. I mean, he makes sure that when he's filming the two guys whatever they gonna be doing, he makes sure the camera sees the two guys taking the condom and opening and putting it on, so they're real safe and all that.

MC: So they'll show that right in the movie?

Apache: But I mean, that part is not in the movies. He films it, so it's legal for him to film it. He films it, but that part won't come out in the movie. You go to a peep show, you go into a peep show, you put in a quarter, they ain't gonna show a guy puttin' on no condom.

MC: So they have to do that while they're filming and then they edit it out.

Apache: Yeah, while they're filming but then they take it out. It's like, you have to be legal about it, you know.

MC: Why do a lot of guys do these movies?

Apache: Well most of them are gay, but a lotta guys want the money. I hear all the time about guys bitching about not gettin' a percentage and how Richie is making money off them. Listen, Richie is makin' money off them, but so are a lotta people. He's the one who has to pay for all this stuff, it's his money, and there ain't nobody puttin' no gun to nobody's head to do it either. All these guys out here who bitch about it, you don't hear them complain about how the drugs they bought are stepped on and full of all kinds of shit, right? You don't hear them motherfuckin' the dealer right? But they bitch on Richie. They bitch, but most of them have still done it.

According to the boys, peep show clients like to seek out and solicit the actors of the movies they view. Raul states: "It's like they think they rubbin' elbows with a celebrity or somethin'. I mean, they see the movie and then find the hustler and try to act out their fantasies with them like they in the movie or somethin'. They get off on it." I had a chance to talk to Richie on a few occasions and his description and assessment of his business tended to verify what Apache and Raul had had to say about it:

Richie: Most of the guys come in here thinkin' they're gonna be stars and make millions. It ain't like that. When they find out how much I pay, some of them want a percentage of the profits. I tell 'em, who do you think you are, Sly Stallone? This is what I pay and that's it—you want it fine, if not, I got plenty of guys willing to do it. Some of these guys amaze me.

THE NORMS OF HUSTLING

From the various types of activities to the movie-making ventures, a pattern to hustling exists to which all of the participants respond. There are agreed-on locations, a familiar dialogue, and a roughly established pricing policy for the various activities. This pattern fosters stability in hustling. For the most part, very few problems occur either between the hustlers and the clients or among the boys themselves. In the vast majority of cases, the activities are completed without incident.

These patterns of behavior can be seen as a normative system that regulates the boys' behavior. One extremely important norm states that once a hustler and a client begin a conversation, another hustler should never intervene. This serves as a type of territorial marker that is not to be encroached on. A violation of this norm can lead to a severe and violent retaliation.

> *Flacco*: You see, that's one thing among hustlers. You don't go and ask nobody, even if you are asking the hustler for money, you don't do it in front of the trick. You don't do that. You don't do that. This one kid caught a serious beat down from me around the corner for that. I had this one trick, he was gonna give me $75 just for hangin' out with him and man, he was about to step off and get into the van to go to New Jersey. This hustler walks up and asks the guy for fuckin' ten dollars, man. In front of me! And I looked at him and said, "Yo you should have never done that." And the trick got all roust [upset] and this and that, and he said to me, "Look, I'm sorry, I just don't like people asking me for money." And he stomped away all pissed off. I turned around and said, "Listen, first of all, you need money you come and see me. But don't you *ever ever* get in front of one of my tricks." And then I kicked the shit outta him so he would never forget that.

Another related norm involves time and etiquette. There are times when a hustler and a trick cannot complete a transaction because of price, type of activity, or some other reason. When this occurs, another hustler may offer his services to the man, provided he waits until this initial conversation has clearly ended. This is often referred to as the client becoming a "free agent." Playboy explains:

> Yeah, well, it's like this. See, if Flacco is talking to this guy but they can't work it out, the guy or Flacco starts to leave. As long as he [the guy] is far enough away so that everybody knows he ain't goin' with him [Flacco] then the guy is a free agent and can negotiate whatever deal he wants with anybody else. I can go up to him now and there's no problem 'cause Flacco ain't got no claim on him, see? That's what we mean by free agent. But I gotta make sure the guy ain't comin' back to Flacco before I approach him, else I'm gonna get my ass kicked. I do that by waitin' until he is far enough away, and then, maybe, I ask Flacco what's up.

Parenthetically, no one can give the exact amount of time or distance that must separate a client from the hustler in order for the client to qualify as a free agent. There seems to be an implicit understanding about how far is "far enough." In all likelihood, the longer another hustler waits and the further the client is from the initial contact, the less chance that the norm will be violated.

Another important norm has to do with preserving and enhancing one's reputation within the community. While street reputation is always important in these circles (e.g. being able to handle oneself, showing courage, and bravery), a boy's hustling reputation is also quite important since it has far-reaching implications. A cardinal rule among the boys is to never allow a client to publicly humiliate or insult them in front of their peers. Public insult leads others to believe that the particular hustler is weak (which can lead to a loss of status and a violent retaliation by the group), and it also serves as a reminder to other hustlers that they, too, could be treated in this way. Additionally, an incident such as this sends a message to clients that public humiliation of the boys is acceptable behavior. Thus, if a hustler does not respond to a challenge to his reputation, it has serious ramifications for him and his social standing. Moreover, it threatens the very structure and social order of the community.

Canno: See, around here your reputation isn't everything, it's the only thing. If I let some fuckin' trick come in here and take advantage of me in front of everybody, then I'm lettin' myself down and I'm lettin' everybody else down, too. They be thinkin' I'm nothin' but a punk, and now I got to deal with them tryin' to get over on me. And every trick that sees this happen starts thinkin': "Hey, why don't I do that too? He got away with it, so why can't I?" So everybody has got to get involved now if I don't deal with it first. But it's better just to not let it ever come up in the first place.

Watchdog: I'm gonna tell you a little story. This is a story about a guy, I ain't gonna tell you his name. He likes to go out with guys and screw them and then gives them twenty dollars. So he walked up to me this morning, he never walked up to me before. He come up to me and asks me what I like to do. So I said: "Listen, first of all, you see me this morning, I cost a hundred dollars. Second of all, this morning, I don't get screwed, I don't get screwed, I never got screwed by no asshole like you." So he starts talkin' all this shit. So I tell him, "Listen"—and before he even told me about the twenty dollars—so I told him, "If you think you gonna pay me twenty dollars for me to get screwed, you must be outta your mind."

So he gets all offended and starts talkin' shit to me about how he could do what he wants to me and all this shit. Then he called me a motherfucker. Well, that was it. He did this right in front of everybody, thinking everybody gonna be laughin' and shit and on his side. Well it got real quiet all of the sudden up here. So I walk up to him, and get right in his face, and ask him real quiet what he said. He looks around, and now everybody be lookin' real pissed off at him, and he got scared. He be like "Nothin, I didn't say nothin', I was just fucking around, you know." And I said, "Listen, don't be fuckin' around like that around here. So don't say shit like that unless you lookin' to back it up." So now he's real nervous and he apologizes and walks real quick to the escalators. We ain't gonna see him for a while now. But he can't be doin' that shit, especially right in front of everybody.

The relationships that exist among the boys also play an important role in the hustling culture. Some, such as Apache, look on the hustling community as one big family:

> It's really like a family here. Everybody knows everybody else, everybody is basically friends with everybody else, and there's kind of a support group, you know. But it's like any big family of boys: you gonna have arguments and fights, and people gonna get pissed off at each other, but basically we all know what we're about, and if somebody needs something and we know them, we help them out. The New Jacks [new hustlers] are different cause we don't know what they about yet. But after you been here a while and you straight up, you added to the family.

Like brothers, hustlers usually pair off and hang out together, sharing drugs, money, or other incidentals. Moreover, a sense of loyalty and responsibility develops between each boy and his partner whereby they will try to protect each other. When one boy goes with a client to a hotel, for example, his partner will usually wait either outside the room or at the hotel entrance.

In some cases, however, a hustler's partner is not always available. In those instances where a hustler has been picked up by an unknown client, there is an understanding among the members of the community that the boy will not go with him alone. There is usually someone who is hanging out or has just returned from a sexual exchange who can accompany the hustler. What is significant about this norm is that it also includes situations in which a hustler will sacrifice his own opportunity to turn a trick in order to protect his comrade. While I believe that this norm emerged as a means of survival rather than due to altruism, it is an important element in the nature of the trade.

Admittedly, I had some initial difficulty understanding this rule. The streets are a desperate place, and this particular type of street life seemed, at first glance, particularly problematic for the participants. However, one must recognize that many hustlers engage in the trade only to supplement their income. As a result, a number are not involved in the mad scramble to earn every single dollar they can. In fact, in some cases, their situation allows them to forgo economic advantages in the name of maintaining strong social ties.

Consider Eddie and Jose's relationship. Eddie always goes with Jose when the latter takes a client to a nearby hotel. He waits outside the main entrance to ensure that Jose comes out safely, and Jose, in turn, does the same thing for Eddie.

Jose: This thing? It's a job, a constant job. You eat off it, you get clothes off it, you get drugs off it, you meet a lotta people, but you gotta know what you doin' or else you gonna get hurt. Every day somethin' happens. Every day me, him, everybody runs into somebody. Either, "Yo you wanna get high, you wanna make a few dollars, you wanna go eat and make a few dollars, let's go." It happens, it happens. I turned Eddie on to a steady of mine. And every time the steady sees him, he throws me some money, maybe five or ten dollars. We know which ones pay more than others. Like if a guy wants me, and he looks at me and he looks at him, I know him, I tell him, "Yo that guy is $35 take him." Or he'll tell me, "Yo what is that date like; no, that nigger fucks you," or I'll tell him, "No, don't go with him he wants you to suck his dick." So, boom, I'll let him know.

Eddie: You gotta be careful of tricks, though. They be like, "No you didn't do the job right," so you gotta get really, really uptight sometimes and perform in there: "I'm gonna beat the shit outta you, you're not leavin' this room." I usually bring [Jose] with me. He gets picked up and I see him go into a hotel, I'll wait in front of the hotel. Like if you go to their apartment and they do somethin' there, some of these guys, they gotta realize they gotta pay.

Like this one Japanese guy I had the other day. We were in the booth, you can go in the booths with these guys. Well this guy didn't think he had to pay cause we went in the booth together. I took this guy and lifted him up by his neck in the booth and took his money. He didn't think he had to pay. So for not payin' me the twenty dollars you owe me, I'm takin' your wallet. That was a hundred and fifty dollars, his quarters, and a lottery ticket. He was cryin' over that. I took his phone card, too and brought it to the Port, and sold it for $35. And where was my boy? He was

right outside the booth waitin' to see if I needed him. We
got high that night [high fives partner].

This issue of loyalty also emerges when conflict arises. For instance,
when conflicts and fights occur, it is expected and even demanded, that
a hustler's friends, and especially his partner, come to his defense. The
issue of who's right is irrelevant; the only concern is how many friends
will be fighting alongside him when fists fly.

For instance, one day Angel began arguing with another male in
front of the bus terminal. As is often the case, in a matter of minutes,
the situation escalated into a brawl. The other young man had three
associates with him, whereas Angel had only one companion, Nelson.
Given the strong police presence in and around the area, the fight
began and ended quickly. However, Nelson had failed to join in to
support Angel. Raul and I were walking down 8th Avenue when we
saw what was happening. Running to the scene, Raul became furious
when he learned Nelson had not reacted:

> *Raul*: That stupid son of a bitch! What is this bullshit about
> him bein' on parole? That's fuckin' bullshit! If I see my boy
> is gettin' a beatdown, and that's my real boy, you think I'm
> on parole, I can't do nothin'? I'm gonna jump on the moth-
> erfucker even faster cause I know I'm goin' to go back
> upstate. He's talkin' about bein' on parole. I be like, 'Yo
> man, what's up, I thought you were one of my boys,
> man?'' That's when he be gettin' a serious assbeatin'. I
> should kick his ass now in front of everybody just to teach
> him a motherfuckin' lesson. I'm gonna get you man! You
> and me, man!

Thus, the relationships between hustlers have far-reaching effects.
Most maintain close ties with one other hustler while also participating
in the larger collectivity. The trade norms include personal protection
from tricks as well as other outside threats, and a standing rule involves
the importance of sharing drugs or money. If a hustler has one or the
other, he is expected to share them with his friends and associates. This
helps everyone to endure and pass the time. Additionally, as Eddie
mentions, there is an unwritten "book" about clients. Hustlers will
share information in terms of the potential danger and what is expected

in terms of payment, as well as any particular preferences the trick may have.

* * * *

It's Monday and I meet up with Melvin, Eddie, Smokealot, and Doubletake on 42nd Street. The temperature is nearly 60 degrees fahrenheit, warm for the first week in March. Mondays are considered slow since most of the tricks are either at work, recovering from the weekend, or both. By 1 p.m., most of the hustlers can be found in and around the terminal.

The boys are tired, and most of their time is spent standing around trying to shake off the effects of lack of sleep and the ingestion of far too many drugs. Tales of the weekend or, as they put it, the latest "dirt," form the main topic of discussion. A few hustlers have taken the weekend off from prostitution, either to spend time with their families or to recuperate from a long run of late nights. They are usually the most interested in the weekend's activities, since they have missed out on the action.

Mondays, then, are one of the best times to talk and hang out with the boys. They aren't very busy, most are in relatively good spirits, and they are anxious to socialize. Boisterousness and loud banter characterize these interactions as the boys try to upstage one another with tales of exploit and daring or play the sometimes dangerous game of "cutting," or insulting each other. The goal is to see how close they can come to offending another person while still getting a laugh. In many ways, this scene is reminiscent of conversations and horseplay found in lockerooms and schoolyards around the country. To the uninitiated, it gives little or no indication that the weekend's activity involved prostitution.

As we stand in front of the terminal, crowds of people stream by, as do many friends, associates, and tricks. A few stop to say hello and maybe hang out for a few minutes to talk. We stand against the glass wall in front of the terminal, facing 8th Avenue on the corner of 42nd Street. I met the boys here at about one o'clock this afternoon, and we have remained in the general area. A large group gathers, which inhibits passersby from making their way into the terminal. Greetings, consisting of hand slapping and raucous laughter, go on for about fifteen minutes before a Port Authority police officer wanders and tells us to "get lost." At first I think this may lead to a reaction of moans and complaints, but surprisingly, everyone in the group stops whatever discussion they are having and starts walking toward 41st Street. At this corner the conversation begins where it left off, without any reference to the officer or his comments. Another ten minutes lapses, and then the same officer comes by and tells us to "move it." Again the group simply picks up and leaves, walking to 40th Street on 8th Avenue with no mention made of the officer. During this conversation, different people come and go, either to hang out at the Meat Rack, pick up a trick, or continue on their way. However, a crowd always attracts attention, and while some hustlers leave, others arrive to see what's going on. Another fifteen minutes go by, and then a different officer comes by and tells us to "hit the road."

Dutifully, members of the group again comply without responding. As the officer leaves, I see him walk by a few individuals who are leaning against the wall or standing in front of the entrance. The officer speaks to some, who then depart: others he simply ignores. The boys who leave simply walk a short distance in the opposite direction of the officer, usually to the next corner. I grow curious about this and ask the group why the officers continue to force the boys out of the immediate area. Doubletake had this to say:

Well it's like this. We know almost every cop in this place. They get new ones every once in a while, and we get to know them too. We know they got a job to do, and they know we just tryin' to make a livin'. So they leave us alone, basically unless we causin' trouble or they get the word to move us. They know that we ain't really about robbin' people around here, cause it's too visible. And we know if we don't move, they just arrest us or write us a summons. We don't need that shit either, so when the Man [police officer] tells us to move, boom, we move. We don't make a big deal out of it, and we don't make him look bad.

His rep around here is important too, so you don't dis the Man. It's the same upstairs, too. Like on the Meat Rack, they got a guy who's up there all the time now. When he sees us, he's gotta tell us to get outta there or he gets shit about it. Hey, no problem, we'll go somewhere else and then come back. We ain't in no hurry, we find tricks everywhere. But he understands what we're about, and we understand what he's about. Some of these guys are assholes who just want to break your balls and call you faggot and shit, but most of them are okay. We get along okay as long as everybody follows the rules, and one of those rules is when he tells you to move, boom, you gotta go right away. You give him any shit at all and you gonna get your ass whipped.

Thus, most of the group's time together is spent simply walking from one corner to the next. We then decide to take a walk to the upper concourse, the Meat Rack. Just beyond one of the departure gates there is a men's restroom on one side and an ice cream shop on the other. In between is an open area in the shape of a square, with escalators at one end leading to the lower level. This is another hangout where many clients come in search of hustlers. If the boys are not found outside or near the Meat Rack, they will be either in this area or in the arcade located a short distance away.

While the bars, parks, and peep shows are hangouts, the terminal is the place in Times Square where most hustlers meet, pass the time, and look for tricks. It is generally perceived as a prime location for making money.

Pretty Boy Tony: This place is like a fuckin' paradise for hustlers. There's always some way to make money. You can pick up tricks, you can sell time on telephone cards, you can carry luggage. There's always somebody who's lookin' for something, and they are willing to pay for it. There's people here who need directions, you can give it to them for a buck or two, people want drugs, people want [Pause] everything. You can even sleep here if you know where to hide. And everybody comes here cause they know this is where lots of people hang out, especially in the winter cause it gets cold. In the summer you can't hardly find anybody, they spread out all over the place, but when it gets cold, this is the place to find them.

I overhear Eddie telling Smokealot and Doubletake about his recent arrest. He was arrested for prostitution and went to court this morning.

Eddie: Oh, I hate that shit, man. I go in there at nine o'clock in the morning on a Monday, and the clerk reads

the charge, and like everybody be listenin' and shit, and he
say loud and clear, Section blah blah blah, *prostitution* and
I be like, "Ohh, man." I be like, "No man," tryin' to hide
my face and shit. It's embarrassing. But I got community
service. I gotta go and sweep the motherfuckin'
subways—you ain't gonna be seein' me cleanin' no subways. Word.

In the course of these conversations, the boys engage in one upmanship
when depicting the risks and dangers in their experiences. When one talks
about how exciting a time he had on Friday, he will usually embellish for
the sake of either getting a laugh or increasing the drama. After the others
react, another hustler will then try to upstage the previous hustler with a
story of his own that is more dramatic and exciting.

This continues until someone recounts a story so incredible, that the
others laugh at him in disbelief, thereby defusing this expanding display
of lies. I have watched Apache or Flacco purposely tell a story that is
so absurd that everyone gets a good laugh out of it.

Apache: I do that sometimes [tell an absurd story] because
these guys get so caught up in it. I mean they be gettin'
mad and shit at each other cause somebody made up a story
that was better than theirs. This happens a lot with the
younger guys who don't have their rep [reputation]
established yet. So when somebody else comes in and tells
a better story, they feel that person made them look bad and
they get pissed off. So I keep an eye on them, and if it's
gettin' like that, I'll tell them a story that's all fucked up,
and then we be laughin' and shit, and everybody forgets
about it and goes on to something else.

A great deal of time is spent hanging out and doing very little. This
became apparent to me the first day I spent with the hustlers. I looked
at my watch expecting to find that it was almost time leave, only to
discover that a single hour had passed. It took some time to get used
to the slow pace. In an attempt to offset some of the boredom, the boys
often panhandle to acquire enough money to buy food, cigarettes or
beer at the small convenience store near the corner of 41st Street and
8th Avenue.

Today, Doubletake solicits the commuters for money and collects almost three dollars in about fifteen minutes. Eddie does the same thing and comes up with a dollar fifty, while Smokealot is only able to raise a dollar. Pooling their money, we walk over to the store where they buy cigarettes and a "forty," a forty-ounce bottle of beer. "Have any of you guys eaten today?" I ask. "No," they reply in unison. "Have you?" Doubletake asks me, and I realize I have not had lunch yet either. "I only have a few bucks on me, but pick out something to eat," I tell them. The small counter is covered with cup cakes, cookies, and potato chips—a junk food junkie's feast. I buy a prepackaged muffin, and we all head outside. Since it is warm, we stand in the sun and eat. The food is consumed with dizzying speed, partly because of hunger but also because the boys want to drink the beer while it is cold.

Since Doubletake earned the most money, he is given the bottle first (after we have all tapped the bottletop with our palms for good luck). He opens the bottle and makes a small X on the ground with beer as a tribute to those who have either died or have gone to prison. Doubletake takes the first drink and the bottle is passed around. After handing the bottle back to Doubletake, Smokealot reaches into his pocket and lights up a blunt (a large marijuana cigarette). We are standing on the sidewalk of a busy Manhattan street but he begins smoking it as if he had not a care in the world.

We dodge the traffic on 8th Avenue and walk back to the Port where we meet up with Melvin again. He had left a short time ago with a trick and is now back thirty dollars richer. "Come on man, let's go up the Deuce," he says. As we again cross 8th Avenue with suicidal abandon, Melvin loudly sings the theme to the movie *New Jack City*. "I'm a New Jack Hustler!" he bellows.

As the five of us walk up 42nd Street, I notice that Eddie keeps looking at the storefront displays. I am in the middle of the group, and as we pass a collection of sunglasses on a display stand, I see Eddie casually take a pair off the rack and put them in his jacket pocket. Nobody but me has even noticed what he did. When I smile at him, he realizes I saw the theft.

> *Eddie*: See, what you gotta do is act natural, you go in, boom, you hit it and keep going. A lotta these chumps walk around, looking suspicious, and then they get caught. I just go in and

take it as I go. Sometimes I'll bump into it a little—that way,
they don't see what you did—but you gotta be cool about it.

We continue strolling up 42nd Street until we reach the Crossroads
Block and then cross the street and head down the other side. We look
at the movies that are playing and windowshop much in the same way
that thousands of others do each day. We stop in front of the Liberty
theater, which is showing the movie *An American Me*, a story of
Hispanic inmates inside a maximum security prison. Since everyone in
the group is Hispanic and everyone has spent time in prison, there is
a good deal of oohing and ahhing accompanied by claims that they
simply must see this movie.

We return to the terminal and I discover that only an hour has
passed since the boys began panhandling although it seems a lot longer.
We walk up and down the sidewalk in front of the building looking for
familiar faces, tricks, or some type of excitement. Finding none, we go
inside to the Meat Rack and circle around the upper concourse, past the
shops, and into the bowling alley in the south end of the building. We
make our way through a crowd of clamoring young people who are
watching the players of the various video arcade games. So adept are
the boys at these games, that although we spend about a half hour
there, each one spends barely a dollar. They show me some of their
techniques to success, but being a novice, I lose quickly.

We return the way we came and settle once again outside the
building near the corner of 42nd Street and 8th Avenue. A few friends
show up, and once again a crowd gathers. The same stories of the
weekend are recounted, both to the new members of the group and to
those who have already heard the news. Ten or fifteen minutes pass,
and then a uniformed officer tells us to "get lost." The cycle is now
complete. This is how the day is spent, simply moving from one place
to another; acquiring enough money to buy food, beer, drugs, and
other incidentals; then returning to the terminal, checking out the scene,
and seeing who's come around.

One of the most interesting aspects of this existence is its
encompassing nature. Aside from windowshopping or interesting
movie, virtually all the conversations between the boys center on
hustling and related activities. Drug use, sexual exploits, evaluations of
tricks, jail time, and amount of money made are the topics of
discussion. No one mentions sports teams, outside activities, or family.

When the stories of sexual exploits run out or have been heard several times over, the conversation will begin to drag. It grows quiet; and no one really has much to say. This has happened with several groups of hustlers with whom I have spent time as well as with individual hustlers. Discuss the trade and they are loquacious, but they usually do not discuss other subjects or will only talk about them when we sit alone apart from the others. Hustling seems to be the boys' total existence.

I'm standing with Melvin and Doubletake when Lite approaches. I haven't seen him in a while and wonder how he has been. Lite asks me whether I have been to the bars yet. Essentially, the boys frequent only three bars. All are gay bars since this is where most clients can be found, and all are owned by the same individual. The first, Hombres, is just across the street from the Port Authority on 41st Street. It is a single rectangular room, about twenty-five feet long and fifteen feet wide, with a bar on the left as one enters. At the far end of the room is a pool table, two video games, and a jukebox.

Directly across from the bar are two small tables and a large wooden box, which is used by the club dancer/stripper. The box is barely big enough for a man to stand on let alone dance, but then again, dancing is not his primary function. Posters and handwritten signs cover the walls, advertising specials, happy hours, and "cock night," in which the lucky winner receives a date at a local restaurant with the dancer of his choice.

Another bar is located on 42nd Street near 9th Avenue. Called LaFleur's, it is much larger than Hombres. It, too, is popular among the hustling population. The third bar is a small, obscure one, on 47th Street near Tenth Avenue, called Tricks. Lite and I go into Hombres to talk. It is quiet in the bar at this time of the day since the rush hour crowd has yet to arrive. In fact, we find we that are the only people there except for the bartender, Paco. Lite tells me he is having problems with his welfare benefits and wanted to ask me for my help, but not in front of anyone else. He is behind on his rent and his landlord is about to throw him out unless he comes up with the money. Through some sort of administrative error, his check has not yet been sent to him. He explains:

> I just don't know about those forms and shit, man. See, I
> can read, but not too good, so I was wondering if you could
> help me out and get this straightened out for me so I don't

get evicted or nothin'. I told my landlord I was having problems with the welfare people, but he didn't wanna listen. He say, "All I know about is my rent money; you don't pay, you get the fuck out." But if you could go with me and get this worked out, it would be a lot easier.

Lite is a new recipient of public assistance, which may be part of the problem. I agree to go to the welfare office with him and act as his representative. Paco overhears our conversation and in a gesture of faith, offers me a drink on the house.

Yo, try this drink man. I heard about it from a friend of mine. It's Jack Daniels and apple cider. No, no, really, it's good. You won't even taste the J.D. Something happens with the cider to cut the flavor. Hey, you know, Lite is straight up. I've known him a while. When he owes people, he pays them. If he's got a problem, he solves it. The fact that he's here asking you says a lot about you. So don't think he's bullshittin' you. He's straight up, man, word.

Lite and I chat a bit longer, and we agree to meet on Wednesday to go to the welfare office. Then we make our way back to the Port Authority. When we arrive I am not surprised to find that most of the boys are still there. I see Raul, who he greets me.

Yo, what's up man? Did I tell you? I'm leavin' tonight to go to Puerto Rico. Yeah, man, I gotta go and get five thousand dollars from my parents. [Couldn't they just wire it to you?] Well, yeah, but I haven't seen them in a while so my mother wants me to stay. I'm leaving at seven o'clock tonight out of LaGuardia. Yeah, man, I'll be gone about a week. When I get back, I'll buy you dinner for a change, alright? [What do your parents do on the island?] They retired, man. Oh, I get it. You wonderin' where got that much money from. I told you about the time I got hit by that cab, right? When they broke my leg and shoulder? [Now I remember.] We settled for twenty-five thousand dollars, and I gave it to my mother and told her to keep it. Cause I knew that if I had it here, I'd spend it all. Plus, if the city found out I had that kind of money, I'd lose my welfare. So now, if I really need it, I have to go to Puerto Rico to get it. So I don't spend it so fast. But I'll be back next week and we'll go to dinner. I know this great place where they serve the best seafood in New York.

That was the last time I saw Raul. A week later, I found Melvin, Eddie, Mad Max, Apache, Flacco, Uzi, and Smokealot sitting on a bench in a park on 43rd Street. They looked up at me and their somber and pained expressions immediately told me that something very bad had happened: Raul had been robbed and murdered in the Bronx the night after he returned from Puerto Rico. There were many rumors about what happened and why, but the general consensus was that Raul had gotten into trouble with drug dealers.

Apache: Yo, man, they killed him. He was tellin' people he was going to get five grand from Puerto Rico. He was stupid. He even showed people his plane ticket. It was like he had to prove he was goin' or something. Tellin' people he was comin' back with five thousand dollars, what a stupid motherfucker. See, and the thing is, he was gettin' back into dope again. He was clean for a while, but I know he was usin' it again. And when he was usin', he used a lot, too, man. It had to be drugs, man, the way they killed him—a bullet in the back of his head—they was tellin' people something. It was a warning, like don't fuck with us, man. He must have got in trouble with some dealers and that's why he went to get some money, but by then it was too late. They took his money and killed him anyways.

Flacco: Yo, how do you know, man? Did you see the body? How do you know he got a bullet in his head? I heard he got shot but it wasn't by no dealers, bro. He was carrying a lot of money; any homeboy could have done him in. He was tellin' everybody how much money he was gonna bring back. All they had to do was wait for him. And you know he wouldn't let no motherfucker get behind him, he was too smart for that. He would have fucked them niggers up good. No, he would have gone down fightin'.

Melvin: Aw man, how do we know it had anything to do with drugs or the money? How do we know it ain't some mother-fuckin' crazyass trick that offed him? Ain't none of us seen what happened. Ain't none of us seen the body, we don't know shit. And you think Raul was dumb enough to carry five grand in cash around with him? No way, man! And if it was some trick, he'd have to be real smart or real strong to do Raul.

There is a difference of opinion within the hustling community about what exactly happened to Raul. Some think the death was drug related, while others think the murderer was an insane client. Regardless, however, his death sent shock waves through the community. There was a discernible tension between the boys and clients and among the boys themselves for a long time after this event. While almost every hustler generally carried some type of weapon (either a knife, a straight razor, or Mace), many began carrying handguns as well. This was based on the idea that if Raul had died at the hands of a crazed or sadistic client, they did not intend to be the next victim.

This period of heightened tension and anxiety lasted for about a month. By April, Raul's death was no longer a topic of discussion. It had become a simple reminder of what can happen to someone who lives the life of a hustler. However, this period was a very difficult one for me. With an increased number of hustlers carrying firearms, coupled with the nervous tension that arose when people approached them, I felt there might be some cause for concern. I did not want to find myself in a situation where I said the wrong thing to someone and suffered violent consequences as a result.

I talked to Apache and Flacco about it and they advised me to tread softly and, if anything, to be seen more because if I departed from the scene, it would appear I had something to do with Raul's death. Their advice was to stick close to them and not ask too many questions of a personal nature. As it turned out, this was sound advice.

Toward the end of March, I met Mad Max, a young crackhead. While Mad Max has a serious drug problem, he is also perhaps one of the most intelligent hustlers I have met. He was exceptionally helpful in understanding one of the most important influences in the hustling culture: crack. The drug and its effects have caused a number of conflicts among the boys as well as many changes in the hustling culture. This influence is the topic of the next chapter.

5

Cracking the Code

It's Wednesday afternoon, and as I wander around the Port Authority, Mad Max sees me and approaches. I have not seen him in quite a while, and I wonder how he has been doing. Max introduces me to his friend, Panhead. We stand around for a few minutes watching people pass by until Max tells me that he and Panhead are about to go to "cop" [purchase] some crack. I ask him if he is still working for the Colombian drug dealers who hired him a short time ago but he becomes reticent: he does not want to discuss the matter in front of Panhead. He shakes his head and quietly tells me that he will explain later.

We leave the terminal and head to what Max describes as his favorite copping zone. When we get there, Panhead and I wait on the corner across the street. Panhead recently arrived in the city from Panama; he met Mad Max while hanging out at the terminal. The two quickly became friends, and Mad Max has been "schooling" him on New York City street life. Max returns with two other young men and I that think something has gone wrong, but the men are simply colleagues that he encountered on his way back from the copping zone. They are about the same age as Max (eighteen), and they introduce themselves as Lupo and Pedro.

We walk to 39th Street near 9th Avenue and continue until we find a side street with little traffic. I stand on the corner while the four men walk halfway down the street and huddle in a doorway to get high. They return quickly and I soon notice Max growing increasingly paranoid, looking constantly around in search of a potential threat. Lupo and Pedro leave, and the rest of us go to find a public telephone, where Max calls his mother in Puerto Rico. He begs her to send money, and surprisingly, she agrees. He comments that she rarely has

any money to send him, and when he calls she generally pleads for him
to return to the island. Today, however, his mother agreed to wire him
fifty dollars within the next hour or so. Hanging up the phone, Max is
ecstatic. "Yo man, she did it! I can't believe it! She never have any
money to send me. Yo, I'm gonna get me some food, buy me a redtop,
word! Yo, Bob, I owe you too man. I'm buyin' you lunch this time.
Word." As we walk over to the Western Union branch on Broadway,
Max comes down from his high. Panhead has remained quiet
throughout the time I am there. At first I think he is leery of me or
misunderstands my relationship with Mad Max, but I discover later that
it has more to do with his limited knowledge of English than trepidation
or wariness.

After Mad Max receives the money, we head to a local fastfood
place where we have a chance to talk. There I ask Max about the crack
trade and his role in it.

> Well, Yo, it's like this. Do you know what crack is? Yeah
> you know what time it is [streetwise]. But check this out,
> I'll tell you all I know about it, and then people who read
> your book will know, too. Okay, so it's like this, crack is
> really crack cocaine. You heard of free base? Well it's like
> the same thing. Free base, crack, crack free base, there
> ain't much difference. What they do to make the stuff is to
> take regular cocaine, you know, the powder, and then they
> add baking soda and cook it in hot water, and then they let
> it cool off, you know. When they do that, it turns to rocks.
> They chip off the rocks and put it in these glass containers,
> like this one see? And they use different color caps so you
> know who you're buyin' from. Like, say, I buy from a guy
> that sells purple top. I know that when I buy from him I
> ain't gettin' ripped off or nothin' cause the purple top is his
> marker. Like, there's purple top, red top, green top, yellow
> top, every fuckin' color. And the size of the rock you buy
> depends on how much it costs. So, like, they have jumbo
> rock, which is, like, twenty dollars, or you can buy nickel
> rock or dime rock. You could get a nickel rock for, like,
> three dollars around here, but usually it's, like, five.
>
> See, but crack ain't the only drug around here man.
> They's all kinds of stuff, whatever you want, you can get.
> But most of the hustlers will do, like [Pause] they smoke

their pot, some do dope [heroin], and a lotta them drink
beer, you know, like when we went and got a forty? Word.
Just about everybody I know will drink a forty. But crack
is my drug, man. I still smoke and drink but I don't do
dope, and I loves my crack.

For the most part, Mad Max is correct in his assessment of crack;
however, a few claims in his description deserve elaboration. Additionally, the crack/prostitution phenomenon is an intriguing one,
particularly among this population. Most of the research on what is
known as the "sex for crack" phenomenon centers on female
prostitutes and little if anything is known about how it affects the boys
of Times Square and their hustling activities.

CRACK IN AMERICA

In the mid-1970s the American public was exposed to a relatively
new practice among heroin users which involved intravenous use of a
mixture of heroin and cocaine, known as a "speedball" (Inciardi
1992). At about the same time, another, more powerful technique for
cocaine use was developed called freebasing.

Freebasing involves changing the salt form of cocaine to a pure
form. In the process of preparing freebase, cocaine hydrochloride is
treated with a liquid base such as buffered ammonia or baking soda to
remove the hydrochloric acid. The salt-free, or "base," cocaine is
dissolved in a solvent such as ether, whereby the purified cocaine
crystallizes. The crystals are then crushed and smoked (Lee 1981).
Smoking freebase cocaine results in a quicker "rush" and a more
potent high than ingesting cocaine powder.

Preparing freebase is dangerous because ether (a common solvent)
is highly explosive when exposed to heat. Additionally, freebasing is
expensive since removing the adulterants results in lower quantities of
the drug, and since, over time, users smoke increasing amounts of the
drug. Moreover, the intense high is accompanied by an equally strong
craving to repeat the sensation (Inciardi 1992).

In an effort to address these disadvantages, in the early 1980s a new
form of freebase was developed which became known as crack cocaine
because of the cracking sound it makes when smoked. Like freebase,
crack is processed from cocaine hydrochloride (with baking soda as a

base) and then crystallized. The final product is different, however, because the process removes fewer adulterants and leaves part of the baking soda as a salt. The processing also allows for additional adulterants to be added. Ingredients such as lidocaine or benzocaine, known as "comeback" look and taste like cocaine but produce no high. When comeback is blended with the cocaine powder and cooked, it all remains in the mix. Lidocaine was the first chemical to be effectively used to "step on" or cut freebase (Williams 1992).

A great deal of confusion exists about the differences between freebase and crack and, as Mad Max's description has shown us, even many users fail to differentiate between the two. Freebase is a cocaine product converted to its base form from cocaine hydrochloride after the adulterants have been chemically removed. Crack, on the other hand, is converted to the base state without removing the adulterants. Consequently, crack is not purified cocaine since during the process, the baking soda remains as a salt (Inciardi 1993).

Many users and sellers prefer crack to powder cocaine because of its quicker and more intense high, its concealability, and its high profits. While a gram of cocaine for snorting may cost sixty dollars or more, that same gram can be turned into between five and fifty rocks of crack. These rocks can then be sold for anywhere between two dollars and twenty. Thus, the initial gram of powder cocaine becomes worth almost three times its purchased value when converted to crack (Witkin 1991).

Moreover, crack addicts or crackheads will smoke the drug for as long as they have money. That is, another characteristic of crack is that the user's body is able to withstand vasts amounts of the drug without overdosing (Bourgois and Dunlap 1993). Users quickly develop an insatiable appetite for crack, and three-to-four day binges or "missions," where they constantly either use or search for the means to purchase the drug become common. During these episodes, crackheads rarely eat or sleep.

These missions have a cumulative effect on many addicts' overall state of health and general appearance. For instance, addicts usually ignore the minor scrapes and cuts they encounter on these missions. These injuries easily become infected and cause a host of other complications. Moreover, one of the most recent consequences of crack use has been referred to as the "sex for crack" phenomenon, whereby users will do virtually anything with anyone and for any price, even a single "hit" off the crack pipe.

A considerable amount of literature exists on the association between prostitution and drug use (see for example Henriques 1962, 1965; Goldstein 1979; Inciardi 1993; Ratner 1993; Dunlap and Bourgois 1993; Feldman et al. 1973; James 1976; Friedman and Per 1968). There is also a large body of information on the relationship of cocaine to prostitution (notably Grinspoon and Bakalar 1985; Flynn 1991; Goldstein 1979; Hamil 1970; Rolfs, Goldberg and Sharner 1990; Morningstar and Chitwood 1987; McDonald et al. 1990). However, much of research on the sex for crack phenomenon has been conducted by Inciardi (1993) and Ratner (1993) whose work involved heterosexual women in the crack house setting. One thing conspicuously absent, however, is a focus on male hustlers who become addicted to crack (see for instance Inciardi 1992; Ouellet et al. 1993; Feldman et al. 1993; Boyle and Anglin 1993). The central question, then, is how does the prevalence of crack affect the hustlers of Times Square?

THE INFLUENCE OF CRACK ON MALE HUSTLING

Virtually every hustler uses some sort of drug, and many are polydrug users. One drug of choice is heroin. While most of the boys initially claimed they only sniffed the drug, many later told me in confidence that they do, in fact, inject, it and have, on several occasions, shared their "works" [syringes and related equipment]. Other research on needle sharing among male prostitutes echoes this point (Waldorf et al. 1990). This high risk behavior is exacerbated when crack and hustling are introduced to the equation.

The high from heroin can last nearly eight hours or more. Toward the end of the high, as Goode (1989) explained, users generally become fatigued and begin to nod off while, at the same time, they begin to crave more of the drug. As a result, they must find some way to stay awake in order to acquire more heroin. This is where crack is introduced. The hustler will smoke crack in order to stay awake so that he can hustle to make enough money to purchase more heroin. This cyclic effect of heroin, crack, hustle, and more heroin can go on for days. In some ways it is similar to going on a mission, but instead of constant crack use, there are the added dimensions of the use of heroin and a sexual encounter with a man, both high-risk behaviors, which considerably exacerbates the problem. One entry in my field notes describes how debilitating this effect can be.

Thursday 3/26/92: I see Mad Max on the corner of 42nd Street. He looks very haggard. His clothes are soiled, his hair askew, his eyes extremely puffy. He has not slept in quite a while. As he walks he can barely maintain his balance and his legs bow as if an imaginary horse sits beneath him. He appears delirious with fatigue and nearly stumbles over the pretzel vendor's cart. He recognizes me and begins to make his way toward the wall I am leaning against. He dodges pedestrians and other obstacles and makes it across the sidewalk to where I am standing.

He looks more haggard than he initially appeared. He smells worse: it is an amalgam of marijuana, crack, sweat, and fast food. He attempts to stand as I am, with his back to the wall. He loses his equilibrium and slams into it, whereby he begins a slide to the safety of the sidewalk. He lands in a sitting position and lapses into unconsciousness. As time passes he slips into and out of his mixture of reverie and exhaustion only to mutter something incoherent and fall asleep again. I had seen Max on Monday when he was with a few friends. When the suggestion was made to cop, his response was an enthusiastic "I'm down!" That was the last time I saw him until today.

I have found that many of the hustlers who experience this are younger and have less than two year's experience in the trade. The older ones seem to have either broken out of this cycle of despair or know enough to avoid it. Instead, their drugs of choice appear to be marijuana and alcohol (usually beer).

Canno: These crackheads are so stupid! I try to tell them that this is bad, man, they don't want to get into this. But they don't listen, all they see is the high. But after a while it ain't about no high, it's about gettin' straight. And then when they start doin' crack, they get hooked on that too. Then you see these sorry-sorry-ass motherfuckers chasin' down a trick for a dollar, lettin' themselves get fucked in the ass or whipped and shit for a vial. It's fucked up man. And if that don't get them, they owe so many people money, they get an ass whippin' from somebody who's tired of waitin' for their money. And if *that* ain't enough, they be out here ragged out and shit, starvin', gettin' sick, fallin' all over theyself tryin' to make enough money. You seen 'em. They all over the place, man. But these young, dumb mother-fuckers just won't listen.

In addition to affecting the lives of individual hustlers, crack has also changed the very nature of hustling. While crack vials can be purchased in Times Square for as little as three dollars, many young users are so desperate for another hit they will do virtually anything to themselves or others for as little as the cost of a vial. This sense of desperation is wreaking havoc with the economic structure of hustling. Pretty Boy Tony describes it this way:

See, the hustlin' rate around here has dropped, okay? Because a lotta crackheads started robbin' the tricks, all right? Instead of treating the guy right and doin' the right thing for the guy. But these motherfuckin' crackheads is makin' it harder on me to make a livin'. Like say [Pause] okay. Say I normally charge twenty-five to thirty-five dollars, okay? And then some crack-head comes along, and he all fucked up, well maybe he say he go for five dollars or even three dollars. Now you a trick, what you gonna do? You goin' with the five dollar trick right? Well then how am I supposed to make a livin'? Some fuckin' crackhead come along and charge less than me, and then sometimes they do more than they should for that five dollars. It fucks it up for everybody else.

Thus, since many crackheads are willing to perform the same acts, or even additional acts, at a lower price, many nonaddicted hustlers are losing their foothold in the marketplace. This quintessential example of the free enterprise system does not sit well with many of the other hustlers.

Apache: Yo, man, them crackheads be takin' money outta my pocket and food away from my family, you know? Like I can't feed my kid cause of these motherfuckers, man. They go around takin' tricks away from us. They [the

tricks] come in here and want to save a few bucks, so they
go with the crackhead instead of gettin' what they normally
pay for, man. It pisses me off cause it ruins it for
everybody. Now everybody gots to work harder and shit.

In fact, many crackheads have become so bold they will not only
intervene in a conversation with a prospective client but in a scene that
ironically resembles an auction, will begin to undercut the hustler in his
very presence. This violates one of the most important norms
concerning the hustler-trick relationship. As one might conclude, the
reaction by the nonaddicted hustling population has been angry and
violent. Moreover, the retaliation extends far beyond the individual
disputants.

> *Canno*: Say I'm talkin' to a john, and then a crackhead
> comes along and says he'll go with him for ten instead of
> the twenty I was gonna charge him. So now the john
> doesn't pay me. Now I go to my friend and tell him I can't
> get high with him because I didn't get paid. And he's gonna
> get mad, because now I can't buy drugs and we can't
> smoke pot together. So now we're both pissed off at him.
> And then we tell the other hustlers. We go to them and say,
> "You know that crackhead over there? I had this john and
> he was gonna pay me twenty dollars, but he came along and
> say he gonna do it for ten." So now this guy's gonna go
> kick his ass, and everybody I tell is gonna do the same
> thing. So it ain't just about me kickin' his ass, which is
> what I'm gonna do. It's about everybody who is tryin to
> make a livin' or even knows somebody out here. But they
> don't learn. As many ass whippins as they get, they keep
> doin' it. Some of these motherfuckers got killed, and it
> don't matter to them.

Thus, the community of hustlers is attempting to elicit conformity to
the normative structure by collectively responding to these types of
violations.

While it may appear that the client is benefiting from such an
arrangement whereby the job goes to the lowest bidder, it seems that
crackheads create problems with clients as well. Recall that one of the

most stabilizing elements in the hustling dynamic is that the vast majority of transactions are carried out without incident to either party involved. Crack is changing that. Many clients are being victimized by crackheads.

Some of this victimization involves simply stealing the client's wallet or, after being paid, attacking him and leaving without performing. In other instances, the hustler will return to a client's home, steal his money and drugs (tricks will have often purchased drugs for both of them in these situations), beat him and then ransack the place. As a result, many clients are becoming leery of picking up any hustler.

Crackheads are not selective in their choice of victim, either. While clients are relatively easy marks since they are unlikely to report the crime, crackheads have also taken to victimizing patrons of the various stores in the area, as well as commuters at the bus terminal. This, in turn, has led to an increased law enforcement presence in the area. Consequently, fewer clients are willing to come to these areas for fear of being arrested, which reduces the opportunities for hustlers to make money. Additionally, a greater police presence increases a hustler's chance of being arrested for some other violation.

Crack has changed the nature of the trade in Times Square in another important way. Traditionally, as the boys begin to age or to look older, they become less attractive to clients. This "aging out" process was discussed at length by Humphreys (1970). However, another consequence of crack has been to make older hustlers more attractive. That is, many clients know that if they pick up a young male or one they do not know, he is very likely to be a crackhead. In an effort to minimize the risks of being victimized, many clients now pick up only those hustlers that are older or with whom they have gone in the past. The client derives a feeling of security in part due to having successfully completed a previous transaction with this person and in part due to the fact that the boy is less likely to use crack.

Older boys also reduce the client's legal liability should they be discovered, since both are adults. In short, older hustlers offer clients the stability, experience, and safety they have come to expect. For these reasons it seems that the "aging out" phenomenon no longer applies. If anything, an "aging in" trend is taking place as crack has actually improved the market for older hustlers.

Thus, crack seems to be disrupting the rhythm and flow of hustling. What was once a stable and predictable activity has been reduced to a dangerous and violent scramble for many of the participants. While the violence, or its threat, has always been just beneath the surface of these interactions, crack has brought it to the forefront of the participants' thoughts, concerns, and behavior. Crack has led to the eruption of a price war, long-standing agreements and traditions regarding the trade are being ignored, and the exploitation of clients is causing a shake-up within the hustling culture.

In many ways, these problems and trends parallel those found among female prostitutes, but in some respects, the problems have either become more serious for the boys or differ in degree rather than kind. For instance, while violence is an endemic part of prostitution (see for example Crapsey 1872; Sanger 1897; Woolridge 1901; French 1993), the boys' willingness to, and likelihood of, using violence and victimizing clients is much greater than with female prostitutes. Hustlers can be extremely violent, and they possess the means to carry out their intentions. Additionally, the delusions and paranoia associated with crack use only exacerbate these tendencies.

Moreover, even though rate cutting by heroin-addicted prostitutes has been noted in the literature (Goldstein 1979), the problems associated with crack use are changing the nature of hustling. Many Times Square hustlers are now being forced into acts they would normally consider outside the boundaries of the trade. In other words, these acts threaten their status in the community and their sense of masculinity. The cultural construction of manhood among Hispanics strongly influences their self-perceptions. Given their hustling activities, these perceptions may not be completely clear to them and crack-related sex only adds to the confusion.

Crack also plays a role in the aforementioned aging out phenomenon. Traditionally, as a young boy begins to look older, he is forced to seek other economic opportunities, usually criminal ones. While to some extent men prefer young-looking females, an older female can still earn a decent living through prostitution. On the other hand, until the advent of crack, an older-looking boy would normally find it very difficult to find interested clients. This is what makes the aging in so remarkable a process.

Finally, in Times Square, where a sense of cohesion exists among male hustlers, crack has torn at the fabric of the community and threatened the existing social order. Recall that one of the factors that makes hustling in Times Square a stable and somewhat lucrative activity is the relationship that exists among the hustlers. By coexisting and helping one another, the members of this culture are able to cope with many of the problems they encounter. Crack has become a looming obstacle to the functioning of this community.

*   *   *   *

As Mad Max, Panhead, and I talk inside a sandwich shop, we are constantly interrupted by friends and associates who come by to say hello, ask for money, or try to find a friend, associate, or client. As each one leaves, Mad Max tells me whether he smokes crack and if he is a crackhead. I ask him about his involvement with crack and how his relationships with these people have influenced it.

> *Mad Max*: I been usin' crack for about two and a half years now. I don't call myself a crackhead cause I can still get up and do what I gots to do every day, you know? It's like, I go out on missions sometimes, but they don't last no four, five, six, seven days or none of that shit. The longest I been out has been like two days. But crack-heads, man, they be scandalizin' theyself chasin' the pipe. I don't do that. And I don't fuck up no tricks for nobody around here either. So that's why I ain't no crackhead: it ain't all I'm about and I don't fuck up like they do with the people around here.

> *MC*: So how did you get started using crack?

> *Mad Max*: Yo, check this out. I was hangin' with my boys over on 39th Street where we were before. I was into dope a little then, you know, but we was hangin' out and shit, and then some of the other guys around here started hangin' down there for a while cause the heat was on up on 8th Avenue. So we chill down on 39th by, like, 9th and 10th Avenue till it cooled down, you know.
>   So, like, some of my boys got into smokin' crack, you know, and they was like, man this is some fucked-up shit. And I was like, I gotta try this shit man. So one day when they was smokin' it, I tried some, and we passed it around, you know. And I was, like, freakin' out a little, you know, cause it wasn't like anything I had before. But they was cool about it, tellin' me to chill and shit. I started to get real

nervous too you know, like I was paranoid. But my boys told me that a lotta people get that way when they smoke crack, so that was cool too. Then we started hangin' with other people that smoked, and we met other people and other people, and then we was smokin' all the time. Now a lotta the guys up at the Port be smokin' it all the time too. But they the worst over there, man. I mean they do anything for a hit. I only chill with my boys, and they ain't that bad off, you know. So I guess you could say they introduced me to it and now we hang out, smoke, and just chill.

MC: Do you hang out with them more than anybody else?

Mad Max: I guess I do, now that you mention it. I used to hang out with a bunch of homies who did dope all the time, but I since I stopped doin' dope I don't see them so much anymore. Yeah, I didn't think about that. Yeah I guess I do hang out with these guys more than anybody else. But it ain't like that's all we do. Like, some of us will go to the Port or the peep shows to make some money, and then we might go to a movie or just hang out.

MC: Do you smoke every day?

Mad Max: Every day I can get enough money. Yeah, I usually buy like a vial or two, cause all I need is, like, three dollars for one.

MC: When you smoke do you always smoke with some of these guys?

Mad Max: Well, not all of them, like sometimes only one of them or two of them is around, so we'll cop and then get high together. So, it's not like I only go with all of these guys every time I smoke. Like today, if I didn't see Louie or Pedro, then me and Panhead would have got high ourselves.

MC: How often do you hang out with people who don't smoke? I mean, do you have any friends that you hang with a lot who aren't into crack?

Mad Max: Well, I hang with a lot of people, but most of the time, it's like my boys at the Port, you know, Apache, Flacco, Uzi, you know. But they ain't into crack, so I don't hang with them when I want to smoke. They got an attitude about crackheads cause it's fuckin' up hustlin' over there. So I go there and chill with them, and maybe smoke pot or drink beer, but I don't do no vials around them. When I wanna smoke, I hang with some of my boys on 39th Street or maybe some of them in the Bronx. They cool about it, you know. And that's how it is with most people. If you a crackhead and you hang out at the Port Authority, you hang with other crackheads cause they know what time it is. But if you try to hang with the others, they don't want nothin' to do with you.

This conversation with Mad Max is very revealing. He does not realize that his comments describe the universal nature of drug use among hustlers in Times Square. In numerous conversations with other hustlers about their drug use, the thread that ties these descriptions together is reflected in the explanation given by Mad Max.

By his own admission, part of Mad Max's crack use began when he became a part of a drug-using subculture whose members taught him not only how to enjoy the effects of crack, but also to accept the values and expectations of other users. As he became more immersed in this culture, these values and norms became increasingly important to him, as did his compliance with the group's behavioral expectations. Mad Max frequently hangs out with crack users, and he smokes almost every day. As a result, his contact with drug users is frequent; he was introduced to crack through drug-using friends, whereby his drug use escalated; and he strongly feels that as long as he is not hurting anyone but himself, his crack use is acceptable. He is, in short, a member of this drug subculture.

There is a great deal of controversy surrounding the explanations for initial involvement in drug use, escalation to more serious drugs based on the social interaction within a subculture, and the socialization that takes place within these groups (see for instance Kandel 1980; Kandel, Kessler and Margulies 1978; Elliot, Huizinga and Ageton 1985; Newcomb and Bentler 1988; Jessor and Jessor 1977; Fagan and Chin 1989; McDonnell, Irwin and Rosenbaum 1990; Hamid 1990; Maloff et al. 1979; Zinberg 1976; Waldorf 1976; Becker 1963). No attempt will be made here to resolve the debate. However, what is important for our purposes is that regardless of which explanations are used, there can be little doubt that Mad Max's drug-using behavior is strongly influenced by the group with which he most closely identifies. Perhaps more important however, Mad Max is not affiliated with only one subculture. He is a member of the heterosexual hustling culture in Times Square as well, and attempts to abide by its rules and expectations as well. He is also very cautious about keeping the two groups separate, since they are at odds with regard to crack use.

This issue of multiple affiliations with groups that are in conflict is particularly problematic. Mad Max must alter his behavior and belief systems depending on which group he is with at the moment, and the role conflict that he experiences bothers him at times. His ability to convince others that he is not under the influence of crack is important since the suspicion can have a devastating effect on his standing in the hustling community. He is not yet a crackhead, but in all likelihood he will become one, whereupon the issue of affiliation will become very important. By that time, Mad Max will probably be so caught up in the desperate search for the drug that he does not even notice. To heavy users, crack is the only thing that matters, and violating the norms of the community, ignoring personal safety, and engaging in a host of high risk behaviors are of little consequence.

The rest of the boys in Times Square will have to make a similar choice. If they are lured into crack use, and especially if they have become a part of the hustling community, their social standing in the group will inevitably change. On the other hand, it is possible that the existing normative system may prevent some of them from becoming involved in the crack scene. There will be a few, like Mad Max, who will attempt to manage both worlds, but almost all the boys will have to make a choice. In any event, the importance of the values of the group and the socialization process that takes place plays a central role in assessing crack use among hustlers.

Crack exacerbates the risks many users will engage in—especially sexual risks. The sex for crack phenomenon is relatively new, and researchers give male hustlers only peripheral mention due to a more concentrated focus on females. All hustlers, whether or not they are addicted to crack, engage in extremely risky ventures. The most notable is the risk of infection with the HIV virus, the topic of the next chapter.

REFERENCES

Becker, Howard. 1963. *The Outsiders: Studies in the Sociology of Deviance.* New York: The Free Press.

Bourgois, Phillipe, and Eloise Dunlap. 1993. "Exorcising Sex-for-Crack: An Ethnographic Perspective from Harlem." In Mitchell Ratner ed. *Crack Pipe as Pimp*, 97-132. New York: Lexington Books.

Bourgois, Phillipe. 1989. "In Search of Horatio Alger: Culture and Ideology in the Crack Economy." *Contemporary Drug Problems* 16(4):619-50.

Boyle, Kathleen, and Douglas M. Anglin. 1993. "To the Curb: Sex Bartering and Drug Use among Homeless Crack Users in Los Angeles." In Mitchell Ratner ed. *Crack Pipe as Pimp*, 159-186. New York: Lexington Books.

Crapsey, Edward. 1872. *The Nether Side of New York.* New York: Sheldon Publishers.

Elliott, D. S., D. Huizinga, and S. Ageton. 1985. *Explaining Drug Use and Delinquency.* Beverly Hills, Calif: Sage Publications.

Fagan, Jeffery, and Ko-lin Chin. 1989. "Initiation into Crack and Cocaine: A Tale of Two Epidemics." *Contemporary Drug Problems*, 16(4):579-618.

Feldman, Harvey W., Frank Espada, Sharon Penn, and Sharon Byrd. 1993. "Street Status and the Drug User." *Society* 10(4):32-38.

Feldman, Harvey W., Frank Espada, Sharon Penn, and Sharon Byrd. 1993. "Street Status and the Sex-for-Crack Scene in San Francisco." In Mitchell Ratner ed. *Crack Pipe as Pimp*, 133-158. New York: Lexington Books.

Flynn, John C. 1991. *Cocaine.* New York: Birch Lane Press.

French, John. 1993. "Pipe Dreams, Crack and the Life in Philadelphia and Newark." In Mitchell Ratner ed. *Crack Pipe as Pimp*, 205-232. New York: Lexington Books.

Friedman, Int, and Llana Per. 1968. "Drug Addiction among Pimps and Prostitutes—Israel 1967." *International Journal of Addictions* 3:271-300.

Goldstein, Paul J. 1979. *Prostitution and Drugs.* Lexington, Mass.: Lexington Books.

Goode, Eric. 1989. *Drugs in American Society.* 3rd ed. New York: McGraw-Hill Inc.

Grinspoon, Lester, and James B. Bakalar. 1985. *Cocaine: A Drug and Its Social Evolution.* New York: Basic Books.

Hamid, Alex. 1990. "The Political Economy of Crack-Related Violence." *Contemporary Drug Problems* 17(1):31-78.

Hamil Peter. 1990. "Crack in the Box." *New Age Journal* 7(6):52-3, 109-110.

Henriques, Fernando. 1962. *Prostitution and Society: Primitive, Classical and Oriental*. New York: Grove Press.

Henriques, Fernando. 1965. *Prostitution in Europe and America*. New York: Citadel Press.

Humphreys, Laud. 1970. *Tearoom Trade: Impersonal Sex in Public Places*. London: Duckworth.

Inciardi, James. 1992. *The War on Drugs II*. Mountain View, Calif.: Mayfield Publishing Company.

Inciardi, James, Dorothy Lockwood, and Anne E. Pottieger. 1993a. *Women and Crack-Cocaine*. New York: Macmillan.

Inciardi, James, Dorothy Lockwood, and Anne E. Pottieger. 1993b. *Street Kids, Street Drugs, Street Crime*. Belmont, Calif.: Wadsworth Publishing Company.

James, Jennifer. 1976. Prostitution and Addiction: An Interdisciplinary Approach." *Addictive Diseases* 2:609-18.

Jessor, R., and S. Jessor. 1977. *Problem Behavior and Psychosocial Development: A Longitudinal Study of Youth*. New York: Academic Press.

Kandel, Denise. 1980. "Drug and Drinking Behavior among Youth." In A. Inkeles, N.J. Smelser and R.H. Turner eds. *Annual Review of Sociology* 6:235-285. Palo Alto, Calif.: Annual Reviews.

Kandel, Denise, R. Kessler, and R. Margulies. 1978. "Adolescent Inititation into Stages of Drug Use: A Sequential Analysis." In D. Kandel ed. *Longitudinal Research on Drugs Use: Empirical Findings and Methodological Issues*, 73-97. New York: Hemisphere-Halstead.

Lee, David. 1981. *Cocaine Handbook: An Essential Reference*. San Rafael, Calif.: What if? Publishing.

Maloff, David, Howard Becker, Ann Ronaroff, and John Rodin. 1979. "Informal Social Controls and Their Influence on Substance Abuse." *Journal of Drug Issues* 9:161-184.

MacDonald, Pat, Dan Waldorf, Craig Reinarmen, and Sheigla Murphy. 1988. "Heavy Cocaine Use and Sexual Behavior." *Journal of Drug Issues* 18:437-455.

McDonnel, D., J. Irwin, and M. Rosenbaum. 1990. "Hop and Hubbas": A Tough New Mix." *Contemporary Drug Problems* 17(1):145-56.

Morningstar, Patricia, and Dale Chitwood. 1987. "How Women and Men Get Cocaine: Sex Role Stereotypes and Acquisition Patterns." *Journal of Psychoactive Drugs* 19(2):135-42.

Newcomb, M. D., and P. M. Bentler. 1988. *Consequences of Adolescent Drug Use*. Newbury Park, Calif: Sage Publications.

Ouellet, Lawrence J., W. Wayne Wiebel, Antonio D. Jimenez, and Wendell

A. Johnson. 1993. "Crack Cocaine and the Transformation of Prostitution in Three Chicago Neighborhoods." In Mitchell Ratner ed. *Crack Pipe as Pimp,* 69-96. New York: Lexington Books.

Ratner, Mitchell ed. 1993. *Crack Pipe as Pimp.* New York: Lexington Books.

Rolfs, Robert, Martin Goldberg, and Robert Sharner. 1990. "Risk Factors for Syphillis: Cocaine Use and Prostitution." *American Journal of Public Health* 80:853-857.

Sanger, William. 1897. *The History of Prostitution.* New York: Medical Publishing.

Waldorf, Dan. 1976. *Careers in Dope.* Clifton, N.J.: Prentice-Hall.

Waldorf, Dan, Sheila Murphy, David Lauderback, Craig Reinarman, and Toby Marotta. 1990. "Needle Sharing Among Male Prostitutes: Preliminary Findings of the Prospero Project." *The Journal of Drug Issues* 20(2):309-334.

Williams, Terry M. 1992. *The Crackhouse: Notes From the End of the Line.* Reading, Mass: Addison-Wesley.

Witkin, George. 1991. "The Men Who Created Crack." *U.S. News and World Report*, August 19, pp. 44-53.

Woolridge, Clifton. 1901. *Hands Up in the World of Crime.* Chicago, Ill: Thompson Publishing.

Zinberg, N. E., and R. C. Jacobson. 1976. "The Natural History of Chipping." *American Journal of Psychiatry* 133:37-40.

6

Aiding and Abetting

As I walk down 8th Avenue on a warm June afternoon, I spot Apache heading toward a park near 48th Street. I catch up with him and find that he is on his way to Streetworks Project, a local outreach program that works with disenfranchised or "hard-to-reach" adolescents. "You should go there with me man, you could learn something," he says. I tell him they have refused to help me in the past. "Listen," he says, "you go there with me, I tell them I want you there and that's all there is to it. Because you're with me, they let you in. Then you hang around and listen to what they say and then you on your own. Then when I leave, you leave, it's easy."

We enter Streetworks Project and I am introduced to John, a worker who knows Apache rather well. I learn later he has been helping Apache get his Title 19 or Social Security Disability benefits. John and Apache spend about an hour together, after which Apache is given two bags of groceries: dry goods, canned food, and diapers. He crams these into a large knapsack he has brought with him. Once it is filled, he straps it on his back and we leave. I am a bit surprised that Apache thinks enough of the people at this program to solicit their help and I ask him about this as we talk about his HIV status:

> *Apache*: Listen, that's a hustler's life man. They got somethin' for me and they wanna give it to me, then I'm gonna take it as fast as they gonna give it. That's what a hustler does, man, he takes advantage of his environment. Every time I go there I'll get, like, two or three bags of groceries. That's like every week. Like right now, John's tryin' to get me hooked up with my benefits and that will

be, like, $500 a month. That's good money, it's like a disability in a way, cause of the virus and stuff.

Once he hooks me up with that man, I'm gonna use it for myself. I'm gonna make sure my son and my wife be all right, so sure, I'll put some of this money away and make sure they are taken care of. He's helping me take care of mine. He knows me. He knows all about me. He says: "I know you a hustler I know what you about, man. I know about you bein' in an apartment man." But the way I see it, I don't give a fuck. As long as he can do it, man, I'll take all the money he wanna give up, I'll take it all, man. It's there to help out people who need help. I need help, man!

And the thing is, they think I'm gonna die soon—bullshit! I don't find no difference between me and anybody else. Whether you got this [the virus] or not, you gonna die. I don't believe I'm gonna be in the hospital with no pneumonia and all this shit. I mean, I'll die naturally. I'll die just like you die and everybody else. If I die old, I died. Unless somebody walks up to me and puts a bullet in my head. Yeah, but you see my life is full of this. But I don't believe nothin' about dyin' of no pneumonia and all that shit. I don't believe in that. I mean, the way I look at it, I'm just as healthy as you are. The only thing is that I have something in me that you don't have in you, okay?

This conversation reflects the hustler's life: he is willing to take advantage of almost any situation. Apache's comments also tell us something about the many ways in which hustlers cope with the risks of infection to the HIV virus. While his comments are just one way in which the boys manage these risks, his particular sentiments probably reflect his experience of the initial stages of coping with a terminal illness.

However, a great deal of cultural lore surrounding HIV, AIDS, and how one can become infected circulates throughout the hustling community. Ironically, many of the boys think they are immune from the consequences of these risks and do little, if anything, to prevent infection.

TRANSMISSION OF AIDS

HIV is transmitted when virus particles or infected cells gain direct access to the bloodstream. This can occur through all forms of sexual intercourse; the sharing of contaminated needles; blood, and blood products; and the passing of the virus from infected mothers to the fetus through the umbilical cord or to newborn children through breastfeeding. HIV has been found in blood, vaginal secretions, urine, semen, saliva, tears, and breast milk. While transmission can occur from any of these fluids, tears and saliva alone do not contain a sufficient concentration to cause infection (Hollander 1990).

If a person is infected with the HIV virus, blood tests show the presence of specific antibodies. Antibody molecules in the bloodstream recognize the virus and are formed to attempt to prevent it from spreading. Thus, the presence of these antibodies indicates that an infection has occurred and attacked the body's immune system. AIDS, then, is best described as a severe manifestation of HIV infection (Osmond 1990).

The IV drug user is particularly susceptible to HIV infection. When users share needles, blood from the previous user remains in the needle, syringe, or other parts of the "works." Infection is also possible from sharing other pieces of equipment such as "cookers," which are the containers used to mix the drug, or "screens," the materials placed in the spoon to filter out undissolved drug particles (Inciardi and Page 1991).

Addicts who share but attempt to clean their needles will frequently use hot water or alcohol in an effort to sterilize them. Additionally, rinsing the needle with water also guards against the syringe becoming clogged with blood and residue, allowing it to be used repeatedly. However, a number of studies, such as those conducted by Resnick et al. (1986) have found that bleach is the only effective means to kill the virus.

Perhaps the most common means of transmission for homosexual men is anal intercourse. Other sexual behaviors that have been identified as risk factors including rectal douching, penetrating the rectum with the hand (known as "fisting"), oral intercourse, and the ingestion of semen (Osmond 1990). Additionally, the relative risk of the latter two means of infection are somewhat controversial despite the fact that there is a high concentration of the virus in semen. This issue has not been effectively resolved since there is evidence for both sides of the argument (see Kaslow and Francis 1989; Peterson 1990; Lifson et al. 1990; Osmond 1990). However, people engaging in these acts may become infected by other means. With regard to heterosexual transmission, while use of a condom treated with a spermicide is the standard accepted means of reducing sexual risk, one of the difficulties in reducing heterosexual risk is the subcultural lore surrounding this type of behavior change. The introduction of condoms as a risk reduction measure often leads to suspicion and can damage the relationship between partners. In an effort to avoid such situations, many people simply ignore this precautionary measure (Swanson et al. 1992).

Prostitutes who use intravenous drugs in addition to their frequent sexual behavior increase their chances of infection. The prostitute who is under the influence of drugs when engaging in sexual activity is at greater risk since any precautionary measures that could have been taken will often be omitted. Thus, not only are prostitutes at greater risk of infection than others due to their sexual behavior, their drug use exacerbates the risk.

RISK TAKING AND THE BOYS

With regard to HIV/AIDS, there is little doubt that many hustlers are at risk. They engage in virtually all the primary risk factors mentioned previously and do so regularly. However, many questions arise as to whether the boys know their risk status, and if they do, how they manage to cope with these risks. The vast majority of the boys are quite knowledgeable about HIV and AIDS, and a few take effective precautionary steps. However, there are many others who, while knowledgeable, think they are immune from the consequences or employ inadequate measures to prevent infection. Still others almost passively and fatalistically accept that they will become infected and do very little to prevent it.

In assessing a person's risk, most experts agree that some sort of cost-benefit analysis takes place, but the criteria used and the exactness of this process are unclear. However, they do agree there are essentially five factors that influence risk taking, some of which are external while others are internal. They are knowledge of the risks, proximity to risk, exposure to the consequences of the risks, a sense of invulnerability, and the amount of control people feel they have over their lives (see for instance Wildavsky and Dake 1988; Weinstein 1984;

Kirscht et al. 1966; Perloff 1983; Perloff and Fetzer 1986; Synder 1978).

These factors will be examined in light of the boys' exposure to the HIV virus as well as how they cope with the risks of infection. In some respects, the boys are similar in their risk asssessments to most teenagers (and people in general), but in other respects, their risk taking goes "off the charts." However, the strategies they employ and the decisions they make about their risks have far-reaching implications.

KNOWLEDGE OF AIDS

It seems fairly obvious that if people lack an understanding of the consequences of their behavior, they are less likely to take any precautionary steps than if they adequately understood them. During the early to mid-1980s, the United States made a substantial attempt to increase people's understanding of HIV/AIDS in an effort to reduce their risks. While the base of knowledge increased over time, the hustling population and many other hard-to-reach groups did not learn about the disease, its causes, or, perhaps most important, effective precautionary measures. In 1988, I explored the Times Square hustling population and tried to assess what the boys knew about the disease and what steps they took to avoid it. I found that the hustlers had very little, if any knowledge, of the disease and very little to prevent infection. While a few knew they should use condoms, and even stated that they did use them, none of these hustlers had any in their possession and none could tell me any of the various brand names (McNamara 1991). For instance, Tracy, who was eighteen years old, described the disease this way:

It's Acquired Immune Deficiency Syndrome. Basically it's a virus. A lot of people have HIV virus, which doesn't mean they're going to attract AIDS. You can have the virus and not get the disease. I know it's a deadly disease, and I mean it scares me. I mean it actually comes from people who use [Pause] I mean dirty people who want to lick your asshole, your toes, and all that kind of stuff, that's dirty sex.

It also comes from prostitutes. Women who have sex about twelve times a night and don't wash, and they don't douche enough ya know, and all that bacteria gets stuck up into them, and it creates a fungus. The fungus relates to the blood system, especially if they're not menstrating enough. This fungus, kind of, like, runs through the blood, because once somebody shoots into you, it goes into the blood system if you don't get it out right away. The blood system attacks, and if you don't have enough white and black blood cells, but if you're a whore and all that kind of stuff, your immune system is really not strong enough, so it's not able to get out all those diseases and stuff. The immune system really dies out.

Much of this ignorance has changed, however. There has been a concerted societal effort to reach these types of high-risk groups, especially adolescents, runaways, prostitutes, and drug addicts. Measures to reach these populations include intensive HIV/AIDS education, anonymous HIV antibody testing and counseling programs, and street-level outreach programs (Heller 1990).

Among the hustling population, awareness efforts are well known. Most of the hustlers in Times Square have received AIDS education from at least one source, and often multiple agencies have tried to increase their understanding of the disease and of risk reduction strategies. Consider my conversation with Canno, who told me what he knows about AIDS and how one can become infected.

MC: If someone were to ask you what do you know about AIDS, what is the virus and how does it get transmitted, what would you tell them?

Canno: HIV and AIDS are not the same. HIV and AIDS, there's a line. If you are HIV positive you need to pay attention to your T-Cell count. Your T-Cell count is what fights off the virus. If it gets lower than 500, you got AIDS. AIDS is transmitted in your skin or blood. That's like, people ask me if somebody gets cut and a drop of blood hits your hand, if you catch it. First of all, the drop of blood gets protoplasm, the oxygen. It's dead. The only way you can catch it is straight transmission. Like, for instance, blood transfusion or, once again, sexual intercourse. That's why you use condoms, things are safe with condoms. But that's why I wear two condoms, cause I'm so large, if it breaks, then you got problems. But condoms are not 100%. You can still catch it, but some people use condoms and put vaseline on it.

Vaseline will tear it [the condom] up, that's why you're supposed to use KY [brand] jelly. Because it's a water based jelly. Vaseline is an oil base that breaks it [the condom] down. Another way is people who brush their teeth and they got bleeding gums, and then you give them a kiss. See, light kissing is okay. I haven't heard anything to that nature where somebody had it from kissing or saliva.

You can also get it from drug use. Mainly from people who use drugs intravenously—they share their needles or their cookers or they share their eye droppers. So, they say if you're not gonna stop usin' drugs, you should use your own works, your own cooker, your own eye dropper, or clean them with bleach.

MC: Do you use condoms with everybody you go with?

Canno: Yeah, especially with girls, mainly cause I don't want them to get pregnant. And I love them enough to [Pause] well I wasn't around for four and a half years and I don't know who they slept with. So I wouldn't want to get into that situation again. That's number one—I know what comes around goes around. Number two, because when I sleep with them, I'm sleepin' with all and every one of the guys they slept with and they sleepin' with every girl I slept with. I don't know what they're about. So I don't want to take that chance. See, and if the girl don't ask me to wear a condom, I gotta be worried about what they're about. I mean, if they don't ask me, they probably didn't ask the last guy, and who knows how far back that goes and what they're about?

Canno tells me he learned most of his information from the AIDS education programs offered in prison but also obtained some from the literature available from the New York City Health Department. It is apparent that he does in fact understand the causes of the disease, the means of transmission, and how to prevent infection. While Canno is an adult, twenty-one, and has been exposed to multiple sources, Lite is only sixteen years old, and his knowledge is based only on his conversations with HIV counselors when he was tested.

> *MC*: Assume that I don't know anything about AIDS. If I was new around here and I asked you what is this thing called AIDS, what is it, how do you get it, what would you tell me?

> *Lite*: You could get AIDS from not using a condom. Somebody could be infected and you don't know. You know, that's one way you could get it. You could get it from sharing needles, you could get it from blood transfusions, you could get it without safe sex.

> *MC*: What is it? What does it do, though? What does AIDS do?

> *Lite*: It kills your immune system. It doesn't fight off no diseases that you could get sick at any time.

> *MC*: So do you die from AIDS or do you die from something else?

> *Lite*: HIV is Human Immunodeficiency Virus. Now that's what you get. That's not AIDS. That's just like you are infected with the AIDS
> virus, but not AIDS. And then AIDS will kill you.

> *MC*: So would you say that when you get the virus you aren't neccesarily sick?

> *Lite*: Right! But you don't look sick. You don't look it. Like, I knew this dude that's got the HIV virus for like, eight years and he's still hoppin'. He looks cleans and shit

like that, and he hasn't gotten sick yet. But there are some
people that have been infected for a long, long time that you
can just tell in the face. Or you could tell if their body is
breakin' out with big bumps and cuts and all that shit, that's
one way.

Lite's comments are typical of many young hustlers in the area.
Essentially, then, they know quite a bit about the disease and how one
becomes infected. They know what the risks are, how to avoid them,
and what happens if they engage in risky behavior. This raises an
interesting point about the level of knowledge and risk taking. In some
cases, a risk and its implications may be known and understood, yet the
person may engage in the behavior anyway. Simply understanding the
risks is but one of several factors.

PROXIMITY AND EXPOSURE TO AIDS

Other important factors in risk assessment are proximity and
exposure to risk. If an act's effects or consequences do not occur
shortly thereafter, it often leads people to conclude that none will ever
occur. The longer the delay and the more removed one is from the
consequences, the less sensitve one becomes to their impact. Moreover,
exposure to the consequences of the risks is also an important factor in
risk taking.

Most of the boys have friends or relatives who have been infected
or are suffering from AIDS. In fact, a number of them have told me
they have visited relatives or close friends in the hospital or have
attended their funerals. Thus, AIDS is not simply an abstract idea or
a topic for discussion, it is a realistic part of their lives. Nonetheless,
it does not cause them to give up their dangerous repertoire of
behaviors.

Some people may wonder if the hustlers of Times Square are very
different from most young people their age in terms of their knowledge
of the disease and its effects. In response, one could argue that they
may actually be more knowledgeable since they have received the
information on multiple occasions and often from different sources, and
they have witnessed the effects of the disease firsthand through friends
and relatives who have died from it. On the other hand, the boys also
engage in a wider range of risks and do so more frequently than the

typical teenager. While most of the research indicates that sexual risk is the primary HIV-related issue for adolescents, not practicing safe sex with their spouses or girlfriends is but one of many other risks of infection that the hustlers take every day.

Thus, despite the obviousness and proximity of these risks as well as an increased understanding of the disease, hustlers continue to engage in high risk behavior. For some, part of the explanation relates to their feelings of invulnerability as well as an exaggerated sense of control over their lives. In these instances, the risks are essentially ignored. In other instances, however, they are filtered through the cultural lore surrounding HIV infection. In other words, the steps the boys take to prevent infection are best understood in the context of the hustling culture.

COPING WITH THE RISKS OF INFECTION

The various means by which the boys cope with the risks of HIV infection can be understood by using the framework created by Miller (1958). Building upon Sellin's (1938) work on conduct norms within the context of a subculture, Miller viewed criminal behavior as a function of obedience to the norms and values of a unique and separate lower-class culture. Miller believed that slum areas have a distinct cultural climate which remains stable over long periods of time. The reason is that the people in these areas are unable to succeed in the mainstream culture, and consequently, a group of value-like "focal concerns" evolve to fit the conditions of life in slum areas. He termed these focal concerns Trouble, Toughness, Smartness, Excitment, Fate, and Autonomy.

In these poverty-stricken communities, people are evaluated by their actual or potential involvement in trouble making activity. These acts include fighting, drinking, sexual misconduct, and crime. Getting into trouble is a status-enhancing mechanism. Related to this is an emphasis on toughness. Lower class males also enjoy recognition for their masculinity and value physical strength, athletic ability, and the ability to withstand physical punishment.

Smartness involves the ability to outsmart or manipulate others in the ways of the street such as con games, gambling, and avoiding the police. Smartness goes beyond intellectual skills and places greater emphasis on being able to successfully navigate oneself within the culture. Another important feature of the lower-class life-style is the search for fun and excitement, such as fighting, getting drunk, or causing trouble. While the search for thrills is important, simply "hanging out" is also an important component to lower class life.

There is also a heavy emphasis on fate among the members of this population. Getting lucky, finding good fortune, or winning the lottery is a predominant feature of the lower-class culture. Finally, a general concern exists about personal freedom and autonomy. Being under the control of authority figures such as the police, teachers, and parents is incompatible with toughness. When conflicts arise in such groups, the usual response is hostility and disdain, which often leads to additional problems. In sum, Miller argued that by participating in a distinct and separate lower-class culture and abiding by its focal concerns, criminal behavior will be a natural and inevitable outcome.

The importance of Miller's theory is found in his framework of focal concerns. In an attempt to categorize and describe the ways in which hustlers cope with the risks of HIV and AIDS, I have borrowed and modified this theoretical structure. Additionally, because of the cultural lore surrounding HIV/AIDS issues, this framework is used to shed light on understanding why these ineffective strategies are perceived as legitimate by so many hustlers.

FOCAL CONCERNS, HIV, AND THE BOYS

In looking at how the boys of Times Square cope with the risks of HIV, a distinction must be made between those who are aware of their HIV status and those who are not. The reason for this is that this knowledge results in very different behavior with regard to their hustling activities. Table 6.1 was developed to describe the various coping strategies employed by the boys to prevent infection.

For those who are HIV positive, there are essentially three responses: denial, acceptance with vengeance, and acceptance without vengeance. Perhaps the most common coping mechanisms among infected individuals is denial. The boys simply deny that they will die of AIDS. They cannot accept their fate and instead believe they will survive and overcome the disease. Apache is the latest in a long line of hustlers to enter this initial stage of coping. He states that he is going to die of old age and that he is as healthy as anyone else. He views the HIV virus in the same manner as most people view an influenza virus: as

Table 6.1

Strategies of Coping

Knowledge of HIV Status	
YES	NO
Denial	Denial
Accept w/ Vengeance	Smartness
Accept w/o Vengeance	Toughness/ Trouble
	Fate
	Autonomy

something that could be potentially serious but currently is not and rather is essentially a short-term ailment. For Apache and those like him, it is impossible to come to grips with the actual and very difficult future.

While some deny, others accept the fact that they are HIV positive. However, with this may acceptance come an added problem: vindictiveness. Instead of willingly accepting their fate, such hustlers may seek vengeance against clients involved in the trade. Eddie falls into this category. Eddie is only sixteen and is well liked by almost everyone in the community, but once he learned he was infected, his entire outlook changed.

> *Eddie*: I look at it this way. The only way I could have got it was from some fuckin' trick who was infected. I think I know when it happened, but I ain't positive. But it was some fuckin' trick who knew he was infected, and he didn't care about me. He didn't care about any of these people out here. He probably figured, "Since I got it, I'm gonna give it to everyone I can."
>
> Well, when I got it, everything changed. I used to like goin' out and messin' around, doin' drugs, partyin', pickin'

up tricks. It was fun. Then, when I found out how some sick motherfucker gave me the virus and now I got to deal with it—I'm gonna make every one of those motherfuckers pay too. I don't tell nobody I got the virus: you the only one I ever told this to. But I'm tellin' you that since some fuckin' trick gave it to me, I'm gonna give it to every trick I go with. Fuck them—they don't care, I don't neither. It's like they say about payback.

MC: What about all the other hustlers who go with that trick, though? If you infect him, then he goes with them, they get it too, right?

Eddie: That's why I tell everybody I know and like to use a condom and to use one every single time, cause you never know. You never, never fuckin' know. But if they don't listen and they go with somebody and get infected? Then that's their fault: they were stupid. But you know what? Of all these motherfuckers out here, I bet almost all that got it [the virus] got it from some trick that was infected first.

Eddie's disturbing comments reflect a general theme within the community. It is generally felt that the transmission of HIV to the hustling community came from infected clients who either intentionally or carelessly exposed the boys to the virus. Parenthetically, I asked Eddie why he carried condoms if he sought to infect clients. His reply was that he uses them for his sexual partners and also as a negotiating tool: he will ask the client to wear a condom, and the client will usually offer a bonus to avoid using one. In this way, Eddie can charge more and, at the same time, continue his pattern of revenge.

The last response in this category includes those who accept their status and are not vengeful toward others. This group of hustlers is rarely mentioned by the boys, and even then, only in a limited context. These are hustlers who have left the trade and are experiencing the debilitating effects of AIDS. I have not talked to anyone who falls into this category and, judging from the boys' fleeting references to them, they are not a large portion of the hustling population, at least not yet.

In contrast, the vast majority of the boys do not know their HIV status. Of this latter group, a small number of younger hustlers, especially those who have little experience in the trade, completely deny the possibility of infection. This is similar to the perspective offered by Perloff (1983), Perloff and Fetzer (1986) and others concerning feelings of invulnerability. These hustlers also feel that they have a strong sense of control over their lives, which allows them to predict the outcome of events.

Most hustlers, however, use a series of what can be called "focal precautions," and can be generally categorized as Smartness, Toughness/Trouble, Fate and Autonomy. Each of these categories will be examined in more detail.

SMARTNESS

Smartness refers to the ability of the hustler to possess additional knowledge or devise a more effective strategy than others to avoid infection. There are several variations of this technique. Perhaps the most common risk reduction mechanism is a heavy reliance on the ability to identify an infected client. While the boys admit, on one hand, that an infected person can look "clean" and healthy, they also point out that they will not go with a client who looks "sick." This means that if the client has flu-like symptoms, appears to have suddenly developed a medical problem, or looks pale and sweaty, the boys will avoid him. Prince had this to say about his ability to spot infected clients.

> *Prince*: I only go with clean-lookin' well-dressed men. I don't deal with anybody else. And they got to be healthy lookin' or I ain't goin'. They can't be lookin' sick and shit like they dyin' or nothin' like that. Some of these tricks around here look like they be walkin' corpses or somethin'. But, like, if I see a trick walkin' around here and he's healthy lookin' and stuff, and then all of a sudden I don't see him for a while and he comes back? Or, like, if he tells me in conversation he just been to the doctor for a checkup or somethin'? Then I know somethin's up. Or maybe he starts usin' a cane or somethin' like that. He ain't never used no cane before, so why does he need one now? See, so you got to watch the tricks around here real close and you get, like, signs from them if they sick or not.

MC: Do all the tricks look this way when they're infected?

Prince: No, not all of them look like that. Some of them look real clean and shit, too; that's when you gots to be *real* good at checkin' them out. See, I know all the tricks around here and I can tell which ones are sick and which ones aren't.

Prince's comments are typical. He believes he possesses some innate ability to identify infected clients. Moreover, he states that because of his time spent in the trade, he knows which clues to look for. Perhaps more important, Prince states that he knows all the steady tricks in the area. I ask him later if he ever goes with tricks he does not know and he admits that in the past he has.

   In reality, then, this innate ability to spot infected tricks is based on an undefined, superficial assessment of clients. Those who look physically ill are avoided, and the criteria for selecting the "clean" ones probably rests on how much they are willing to pay. To be fair, hustlers do make some type of initial evaluation, and this wariness is helpful in assessing other types of risk, such as the risk of physical injury. However, as much as the boys believe in its effectiveness, their street savvy cannot protect them from the virus.

   Another strategy within this category is to narrow the scope of customers. Many boys state they now only go with clients with whom they have gone in the past. While this tactic is aided by the fact that clients also seek out familiar hustlers due to the problems stemming from crack, the boys will admit that they have gone with strangers who they recognize could be infected. While a particular client may limit his activities to a small number of boys, those boys, as well as the client, are still at risk of infection. Thus, the hustler may obtain a sense of control by curtailing the number of clients he goes with while failing to realize the potentially fatal flaws of this strategy.

   A third approach involves limiting the range of activities that hustlers will perform with clients. Many have stated that they will only engage in passive oral sex with clients, and since they do not believe they are at risk, they are unconcerned either about the act or its frequency. However, recall that oral sex as a means of transmission remains controversial, and the boys are still at risk of becoming infected. For instance, if a client is infected and has sores or cuts on his lips or the inside of his mouth, he may be able to transmit the virus orally. However, and perhaps more important, one must question whether this is the only type of act in which the hustler will become involved. This is especially true for the crackhead hustler, who will do almost anything with anybody for nearly any price.

Fourth, some hustlers take time off from hustling and in this way believe they can reduce the likelihood of infection via the "law of averages."

> *Deadhead*: If you was a hustler, what would I tell you about how to keep from gettin' AIDS? Well, I would tell you to use your condoms and don't go with more than one person a day okay? If you're gonna hustle, don't go with more than one person in a day. That will decrease the odds of you catching it. Sometimes you take a week off being promiscuous. In other words, don't have no sex for a whole week! That way, you cut down the chance of you gettin' infected with the disease. It's like the law of averages, you know? The less hustlin' you do, the less of a chance you have of gettin' it.

Many who use this strategy find that while they refrain from hustling their drug use increases, or may they engage in unprotected sex with a partner, or both. Consequently, the idea of taking time off from hustling as an effective risk reduction measure is questionable. The likelihood of this happening is also predicated on having the financial means to take time off which is something some hustlers lack.

Fifth, some boys believe that frequent testing for HIV is a viable precautionary measure. Scarface believes he is not at risk because he gets tested every six months. Since he has been tested nearly a half dozen times and each time the result has been negative, he feels he does not need to concern himself. As long as he is selective in his choice of clients and is what he terms "careful" about his drug use (in that he cleans his needles with bleach), he believes he is in no danger. When I ask him what would happen if he obtained a positive test result, he states: "That ain't gonna happen, but if it did? I guess it would be time to make some changes in my life-style." Obviously, regular testing does little to prevent infection and only serves to assess whether it has occurred. Moreover, even if an individual has not yet tested positive, if the transmission was recent, he may nonetheless be infected.

TOUGHNESS/TROUBLE

Toughness/Trouble refers to the boy's street reputation or degree of being a "bad ass" (Katz 1989). Here, the hustler believes that his status in the hustling and street culture will prevent infection by deterring infected clients from soliciting him. The idea here is that an infected client would not dare risk the violent retaliation he would receive if he solicited the boy. In other words, the client "knows better" than to try to pick him up. Raul had this to say:

> Listen, man, my game is tight around here. My shit is real tight. Nobody in his right fuckin' mind is gonna come around here and even think of fuckin' with me. I don't care if he's got AIDS or not. Anybody that comes around here knows the rules. And if I find out that any mother-fucker around here is tryin' to infect me or anybody else, they be gettin' an ass-whippin' they won't ever forget. But for me, I don't need to worry about that. Everybody knows me and they know what I'm about, so I know nobody is gonna fuck around and try to get me sick.

Consider Deadhead's comments, which echo Raul's point:

> *Deadhead*: Well I know who to go with, and so I don't worry too much about that shit. And beside I know Zen Do Kai [a type of martial art], so nobody will really fuck with me. I been around here almost a year now and my reputation is set. Don't nobody fuck with me, especially these johns and the other mother-fuckers around here. I had a fight when I first got here, and ever since then, they leave me alone. See, a lot of them think that because I'm white they can fuck with me. Well, they found out the hard way. But now they know, and the johns know not to try any shit with me. The guys that got AIDS won't come around here, and if they do, they know better than to pick me up.

Despite these strongly held beliefs, almost every hustler I spoke with would admit that infected clients do solicit boys in the area. The difference, of course, is that the boys who go with these types of clients are not as adept at identifying them. Boys who cannot spot an infected client are perceived as having less skill, being unlucky, or possessed of a reputation that is not strong enough to serve as a deterrent. Another possibility is that the boy may be a crackhead and willing to do anything, regardless of risk.

FATE

Fate as a strategy is essentially a misnomer since there is an inevitability associated with HIV. That is, a few boys believe that they will become infected and that there is little they can do about it, so they take no precautions. They realize they may have been lucky up to this point but feel that their luck will soon run out. They are convinced of this outcome and thus do nothing to attempt to change it. In some ways, this is reminiscent of individuals who feel they have no control over their environment as in a stressful work situation.

In the same way that coal miners accept the eventuality that a cave-in will occur or that they will develop a physical ailment, some hustlers tacitly accept that they will one day become infected. Thus, while some hustlers will deny the possibility of becoming infected and others will use a series of techniques to negate their risks, this group of hustlers experiences an inevitability to their fate and does little to attempt to control their destinies.

AUTONOMY

Finally, an interesting trend has emerged with regard to condom use. When outreach workers, police officers, social workers, health officials, and others ask the boys how they prevent infection, they unanimously state that they use condoms. While this could be considered a success in terms of awareness of risks, consider what Flacco has to say about this:

> Man, this thing with condoms? That's what they think they're supposed to say. Some guys use condoms, mostly gay guys, but we all know that when somebody comes around here and asks us what we do to prevent AIDS, we say condoms. If we don't, we'll have every motherfuckin'

do-gooder comin' around here tellin' us about how we should do this and do that, and they won't leave us alone. So we just tell them "Yeah, I use a condom with every single trick I pick up and I won't go with them if they don't want to use one." But it's all bullshit. You and I both know that most of these people out here don't use them. Besides, they ain't 100% anyway so a lotta guys figure, why bother?

Thus, while the vast majority of boys state that they use condoms, I only saw one, Eddie, who ever had a ready supply. As Flacco states, most of the hustlers say they use condoms because they think that is what they are supposed to say. Moreover, even though condom use is perhaps the most effective means of prevention for them, even those boys who do use condoms can be persuaded to forgo them if the client is willing to pay more.

Additionally, many hustlers do not use condoms simply because the messenger promoting their use has no credibility. In short, it has less to do with the perceived or actual effectiveness of condoms and more with the status of the person giving the advice. As Flacco stated: "Them workers don't know shit, they just come around here and pass out condoms and tell us to come and see them if we need anything [Pause], like I need them. Who the fuck are they anyway? They gonna tell *me* what I should do?"

CONCLUSION

The risks of HIV infection for the boys of Times Square raises many issues. The problem lies not in awareness or understanding, but in translating that information into behavior. That is, most of the hustlers know what they should do, but because of the context in which this information is given, they ignore it and continue with their risky activities.

For instance, the seeking out of "clean" clients suggests that the boys have at least a basic understanding of the risks, but at the same time, there is an implied sentiment that clean-looking clients are less likely to be infected. This is in spite of the fact that many hustlers know that a clean client could nonetheless be infected with the HIV virus.

Additionally, they know that the only significant way to protect themselves against infection is through condom use, yet they will not use them nor do they listen to the outreach workers who pass condoms out and try to counsel them.

Thus, the cultural lore surrounding AIDS inhibits the boys from taking effective prevention measures. The information concerning AIDS is received but is distorted to the point where the boys can describe the risks but avoid taking appropriate risk-reducing measures.

The cultural influence as it relates to HIV emerges in other ways as well. For instance, when a hustler learns of his HIV status and even begins to experience some of the symptoms, he may actually increase his hustling activities in an effort to convince himself and others that he is not sick. This "face work" (Goffman 1959) allows him to maintain his social standing and avoid suffering the pains of exclusion from the larger collectivity.

*   *   *   *

As Lite and I walk along 42nd Street, he talks about how the area has changed in terms of its opportunities to hustle. He laments about the increased police presence and the "shutdowns," as he calls them, of the peep shows in the area, especially in the 42nd Street corridor. "It's bad out here man, real bad. You seen them closin' off the peep shows on 42nd Street, it only be a little while before they come to 8th Avenue. It's just a matter of time." he says. What Lite is describing, of course, are the effects of the 42nd Street Development Project, Operation Alternative in the Port Authority Bus Terminal, and Operation Safe Corridor, which have focused greater law enforcement attention on crime in the Times Square area. These topics are the subject of the next chapter.

REFERENCES

Goffman, Erving. 1959. *The Presentation of Self in Everyday Life*. New York: Doubleday.

Heller, Karen. 1990. "Educational Strategies to Prevent AIDS: A Rationale." In P.T. Cohen, Merle Sande, and Paul Volberding eds., *The AIDS Knowledge Base*, section 11.1.1. Waltham, Mass.: Medical Publishing Group.

Hollander, Harry. 1990. "Transmission of HIV in Body Fluids." In P.T. Cohen, Merle Sande, and Paul Volberding eds., *The AIDS Knowledge Base*, section 1.2.1, Waltham, Mass.: Medical Publishing Group.

Inciardi, James, and Brian J. Page. 1991. "Drug Sharing Among Intravenous Drug Users." *AIDS* 9:772-773.

Kaslow, Richard A., and Donald Francis. 1989. *The Epidemiology of AIDS: Expression, Occurrence and Control of Human Immunodeficiency Virus Type 1 Infection.* New York: Oxford University Press.

Katz, Jack. 1989. *Seductions of Crime.* New York: Basic Books.

Kirscht, J. F., D. P. Haefner, S. S. Kegeles, and I. M. Rosenstock. 1966. "A National Study of Health Beliefs." *Journal of Health and Human Behavior* 7:248-254.

Lifson, Alan R., Paul O'Malley, Nancy Hessol, Susan Buchbinder, Lyn Cannon, and George Rutherford. 1990. "HIV Seroconversion in Two Homosexual Men After Receptive Oral Intercourse with Ejaculation: Impilications for Counseling Concerning Safe Sexual Practices." *American Journal of Public Health* 80:1509-11.

McNamara, Robert P. 1991. "From Prophylactics to Prayers: The Reactions to AIDS by Juvenile Male Prostitutes." Paper presented at the Eastern Sociological Society, Providence, RI, April.

Miller, Walter. 1958. "Lower-Class Culture as a Generating Milieu of Gang Delinquency." *Journal of Social Issues* 14:5-19.

Osmond, Dennis. 1990. "Homosexual Transmission." In P. T. Cohen, Merle Sande, and Paul Volberding eds., *The AIDS Knowledge Base* section 1.2.3. Waltham, Mass.: Medical Publishing Group.

Perloff, Linda. 1983. "Perceptions of Vulnerability to Victimization." *Journal of Social Issues* 39(2):41-61.

Perloff, Linda, and Barbara K. Fetzer. 1986. "Self-Other Judgments and Perceived Vulnerability to Victimization." *Journal of Personality and Social Psychology* 50(3):502-510.

Peterson, Thomas A. 1990. "Facilitators of HIV Transmission During Sexual Contact." In Nancy Alexander, Henry Gabelnick, and Jeffery Speiler eds., *Heterosexual Transmission of AIDS*, 55-68. New York: Wiley-Liss.

Resnick, L, L. K. Veren, S. Z. Salahuddin, S. Tondreau, and P. D. Karham. 1986. "Stability and Inactivation of HTLV-III/LAV under Clinical and Laboratory Environments." *Journal of the American Medical Association* 255:1887-1891.

Sellin, Thorsten. 1938. "Culture Conflict and Crime." In Social Science Research Council, *Bulletin No. 41*, 63-70. New York: Social Science Research Council.

Swanson, Nancy, Cindy Patton, Robert McNamara, and Susan Molde. 1992. "I'm Not That Type of Client." Paper presented at the Applied Anthropological Association Meeting, Memphis, Tenn.

Synder, Rick. 1978. "The Illusion of Uniqueness." *Journal of Humanistic Psychology* 18(3):33-41.

Weinstein, N. D. 1984. "Why it Won't Happen to Me: Perceptions of Risk
    Factors and Susceptibility." *Health Psychology* 3:431-457.
Wildavsky, Aaron, and Karl Dake. 1988. "Theories of Risk Perception: Who
    Fears What and Why?" *Daedalus* 154:41-58.

7

Riding Out the Storm

Prostitution, by both males and females, has existed for quite a while in Times Square. While hustlers could be found in all parts of the area, some of the prime sites included Bryant Park, located on 6th Avenue, and the 42nd Street corridor between 7th and 8th Avenues. With the construction of The Port Authority Bus Terminal in 1953, another central location for hustling emerged.

Over time, primarily as a result of changes in enforcement policies and civic efforts, the actual locale of the hustling market has gradually shifted toward 8th Avenue. Part of the reason for this shift has to do with the structure and organization of the marketplace: Times Square hustlers cater to a special group of clients who typically enter and leave the city through the Port Authority Bus Terminal. This is what gives the market its diurnal quality. Because of this dependency on the area, changes in the market's locale are bound to be relatively minor.

Nevertheless, changes do take place. One of the most important changes occurred prior to the start of this project. The physical and social conditions in Bryant Park had deteriorated so dramatically that the area required substantial improvements. As a result of the redevelopment of both the library and the park, along with an increased law enforcement presence, the hustling market was driven out of the park and toward 42nd Street.

This led to a further decline of 42nd Street, as well as the 8th Avenue section nearby. In response, the 42nd Street Development Project was founded as a large-scale effort to "clean up" the streets and revitalize the area. City officials hope that the reconstruction of the 42nd Street corridor and the restoration of the area's historic theaters will make the area more attractive as both an entertainment center and a commercial district.

Additionally, law enforcement efforts such as Operation Crossroads and Operation Safe Corridor are designed to reduce crime and make the 42nd Street area safer by increasing police visibility and also through undercover operations. Similarly, Operation Alternative was implemented to reduce fear among bus passengers, target the criminal element, and at the same time, provide assistance to the homeless in and around the Port Authority Bus Terminal.

Finally, law enforcement sweeps of the area prior to the Democratic National Convention in July 1992 led to a large number of arrests as is common in all police crackdowns. This removed a number of hustlers from the area during that time period. Many hustlers were found to be in possession of weapons or drugs during their arrest, while others had outstanding warrants for other offenses. For these individuals, the time spent away from hustling was extended for months following the convention.

Thus, in part due to civic efforts such as the restoration of Bryant Park, large-scale developmental efforts such as the 42nd Street Development Project, and increased law enforcement pressure, by Operation Safe Corridor and Operation Alternative, the market has gradually drifted north toward 8th Avenue.

Additionally, these different strategies have created pressure within the hustling community and at the same time caused a considerable amount of discord about the perceived future of the trade in the area. This chapter examines the boys' reactions to these efforts as well as how they affect the hustlers' place in the market.

THE 42ND STREET DEVELOPMENT PROJECT

Towards the end of the 1970s, when Times Square had declined to its lowest point, city officials, planners, researchers, and the general public raised a number of questions as to what should be done to Times Square. Some stated it should be restored to reclaim its role as a tourist and entertainment district. Others contended that above all else, the area's cultural diversity should be preserved. Still others argued that it should be a commercial district filled with office space and businesses as in other parts of Manhattan.   These issues were being raised at a time when Times Square, and especially the 42nd Street corridor, had become a den for the unsavory and disreputable. Drug dealing was on the rise, the criminal population had grown considerably, and the sex trade flourished (New York City Police Department 1989).

Developed by Mayor Ed Koch's Administration, the 42nd Street Development Project is the largest in the city's history, with costs expected to exceed $2.5 billion. The project proposes the construction of four office towers, containing 4.1 million square feet of space, at the intersection of 42nd Street, Broadway, and 7th Avenue. A twenty-story mart, containing 2.4 million square feet, is also planned for the east side of 8th Avenue between 40th and 42nd Streets. Additionally, a 750 room hotel with retail space will be constructed on the northeast corner of 8th Avenue and 42nd Street.

The project also calls for the restoration of the historic theaters in the area and for a renovation of the subway system to make it more attractive to passengers (UDC Report 1990). The Times Square subway is a vital transportation hub used by nearly 200,000 passengers daily and is the second busiest station in the City. According to the Metropolitan Transit Authority (MTA), approximately 15 million people passed through their turnstiles in 1990. However, the system has many problems in both efficiency and public safety. Improving the subway station is a key component to the project.

For a variety of reasons, in late July 1992 the proposed construction of the four office towers was temporarily suspended (Dunlap 1992). Thus, it seems that the construction of offices, hotels, and other major improvements are not likely to begin any time soon, and while a few minor changes are underway, most of the buildings in the area remain empty and devoid of activity. Forty-second Street has changed from being seedy and tawdry to ghostly and empty. The only consistent signs of life are the police officers who patrol this corridor in an attempt to reduce crime and violence.

OPERATION CROSSROADS/OPERATION SAFE CORRIDOR

In response to the increased crime in the area and in an attempt to help people feel safe when they come to Times Square, the Office of Midtown Enforcement developed Operation Crossroads and Operation Safe Corridor. These two police initiatives are essentially the culmination of long-term law enforcement strategies in the Times Square area. Operation Crossroads was officialy created in 1979. This strategy consisted of maintaining a high visibility in the area, especially during high crime periods. According to Bill Daly, who heads the Office of Midtown Enforcement, this increased police presence served to substantially reduce reported crime in the Times Square area. He stated: "From 1980 to 1985, crime was pretty much under control. We still had some problems, but we were doing okay. Then crack came on like gangbusters and all hell broke loose" (Daly 1993).

Daly's assessment is an accurate one. From 1986 to 1989, the number of reported crimes on 42nd Street between 7th and 8th Avenues averaged 2,292. Moreover, this number steadily increased from 1987 to 1989. This led to Operation Safe Corridor, a modification of Operation Crossroads. The idea was to saturate the 42nd Street corridor with officers, especially during high crime periods, and reduce the number of opportunities for drug dealers, hustlers, and other offenders in that area.

In 1990, there were 1,505 offenses on the street, a decrease of 35% from the previous year. In 1991, there were 1,069 offenses, a decrease of 29% from 1990. Thus, reported crime on 42nd Street was reduced 54% in a two year period (New York City Police Department 1989, 1992). However, the department wanted to go beyond simply making arrests. In the late 1980s, the Office of Midtown Enforcement received a grant to establish outreach programs for hard-to-reach youth. The program, Streetworks Project, was designed to go into the community and provide intervention on drug treatment, AIDS, and a variety of other problems that street youth face.

To a great extent, then, the reduction in crime in Times Square, as well as in the 42nd Street corridor, has been the result of a saturation of police officers coupled with an outreach program to help needy teens. A similar strategy is being employed in the New York Port Authority Bus Terminal.

OPERATION ALTERNATIVE

The homeless have been a long-standing problem in public places like the Port Authority Bus Terminal. It is common to see many people sleeping in the corners, by the stairs, near the departure gates, and in the numerous cardboard boxes, or "cardboard condominiums," erected side by side outside the terminal. The presence of these individuals is said by terminal officials to create a nuisance problem as well as promoting an atmosphere of fear among passengers.

To some extent, there is good reason for passenger concern, but not simply because of the homeless: there is also a sizable criminal element in and around the terminal. Pickpockets, drug dealers, muggers, and petty thieves, some posing as "red caps" [porters], to steal the luggage of unknowing travelers, are common features of the landscape. Additionally, the departure gates, restrooms, and main entrances to the terminal are common places to find hustlers.

In 1991, in response to a number of complaints by terminal passengers and customers, the Port Authority conducted a survey on passenger safety and conditions in the terminal. Thirty-five hundred people participated in the study, and many of the questions focused on passenger fears as well as an overall evaluation of the terminal. From these findings, the Port Authority Police initiated Operation Alternative in December 1992. Operation Alternative is essentially a cooperative model between the police and a social service component. The primary goal is to identify and assist or eject the homeless and other low-level offenders who harass or intimidate passengers, create a climate of fear and apprehension and contribute to the overall poor appearance of the terminal.

This project goal is accomplished by a strict enforcement of the rules and regulations of the terminal. These rules, which have been posted around the terminal for more than two years, prohibit a wide variety of activities, including obstructing pedestrian traffic; sleeping; lying or sitting on floors or starways; changing clothes, shaving or bathing in restrooms; and soliciting money without permission (New York Port Authority Bus Terminal 1992).

When officers encounter a homeless person in the corridors, they ask if the person wants treatment or shelter. For those who accept, social workers from the Manhattan Bowery Corporation and the Partnership for the Homeless, who are funded by the Port Authority and housed inside the terminal, direct the homeless to a variety of other services such as the Manhattan Bowery shelter, soup kitchens, drug treatment facilities and medical services.

In the first six months of the operation, the number of reported robberies decreased 40%; assaults, 23%; pickpocketing, 42%; and luggage theft, 25%. Moreover, total arrests increased nearly 35% and prostitution arrests increased nearly twelve-fold, from 17 in 1991 to 200 in 1992 (New York Port Authority Bus Terminal 1992).

In 1993, the number of reported street robberies have decreased nearly 49% over 1992, purse snatching declined by nearly 77%, prostitution decreased by 33% and larceny declined by 21%. In fact, the vast majority of serious offenses and a large number of nuisance offenses (e.g. trespass, theft of services, harassment, and loitering) all witnessed dramatic decreases since 1992 (New York Port Authority Bus Terminal 1993).

While it may seem that these strategies are successful in reducing crime in these areas, how do the boys respond to these many changes? How has redevelopment altered their perceptions of hustling? Has this affected the sense of community, or is it only one of many obstacles that have been, and continue to be, placed in their path?

THE BOYS' PERCEPTIONS OF REDEVELOPMENT

"Look at all the places that been shut down, man—they ain't that many left," says Paco as we walk down 42nd Street one early Friday morning. Paco is a sixteen year old hustler who has worked in the trade for about a year. He and I met through Mad Max, and today he and I spend the better part of the day together wandering around Times Square. As we walk, the conversation shifts to a discussion of the redevelopment efforts in Times Square. Paco is worried.

> Man, what we gonna do when they shut down all the shops and shit? How we gonna make a living? The peep shows is the way I make my money, you know what I'm sayin'? Without them, I gotta do somethin' else to make a living. This is the easiest way, but if I gotta, I'm gonna do whatever it takes to get paid, you know? Like if I gotta do stickups cause hustlin' has died around here, then that's what I'm gonna do. I don't wanna do that cause if I get caught, I'm goin' upstate [prison]. I would rather hang out, chill, and hustle a few tricks, and everybody's happy. But if they cut that off from me, then [Pause] why they gotta make it so hard on us? All we tryin' to do is survive like everybody else.

Angel, who is eighteen and has been hustling for about a year, stated: "It's gonna be bad around here man, you watch. There is gonna be some serious shit happenin' real soon. I'm tellin' you man, I'm nervous about this. I mean, I know some of my boys already talkin' about rippin' off the people from the theaters, man." Snoopy Snoop, another young hustler had this to say: "Hey, I'm gonna do what I gotta, man.

If they come down on hustlers around here, then fuck them, they get what they get. I don't want no trouble, but if they bring it on, then I'm with that. They wanna get busy, then I'll do what I have to. Ain't nobody gonna take my money away from me, man. I might hustle anyway, but I got to be really clockin' for the man. I don't wanna get busted. And I know that if they really tryin' to catch hustlers, I might do somethin' else for a while.

Paco insightfully pointed out an unintended consequence of redevelopment:

> But see, the other thing about this is, not only will there be more serious shit happenin', but what little hustlin' is left is gonna be *real* competitive. Like if this thing [redevelopment] happens, all the rules is out the fuckin' window. It's everybody for themselves. Ain't gonna be no, "Oh, I'll watch your back for you," or "I won't interrupt you when you with a trick." All that shit is gone. It's gonna be everybody for themselves and fuck everybody else.

These comments express the fears and concerns of many other young hustlers. They think that the redevelopment of Times Square will have a disasterous effect on the hustling culture, the nature of the trade, and will lead to more violence as the boys turn to robbery and other crimes to earn a living. While this is certainly a possibility, older hustlers take a much more relaxed view of the situation. They see the redevelopment strategy as but one of many that have been attempted over the years and one that will be endured like the rest. Consider Flacco's assessment of the situation:

> I look at it like this. They can come in here and tear down all the buildings they want. They can close every single peep show on 42nd Street if they want. They can even put a DT [detective] or an undercover cop by every gate in the Port Authority. They can do all of that. They can even put a uniform on every corner and keep us from hangin' around lookin' for tricks. But it ain't gonna do no good, you know why? Cause that ain't the answer. They can put up the biggest fuckin' office buildings in New York and clean up all the theaters, too. And they probably will. And they will

probably get what they want, people comin' back to Times Square for the theater and shit. But it don't matter. People want drugs, they want sex, they want a lot of things that are illegal. And if they are willing to pay, they'll get them.

Apache had this to say:

There will always be a way to make money around here. If they shut down 42nd Street, right then we just move over to 8th Avenue. A lotta the peep shows that were on 42nd Street already moved to 8th. As long as they make money, somebody will try to run one. And if they spend all that money cleanin' up 42nd Street, we just wait them out by movin' down the street. We ain't worried: they the ones that are worried. See, it's a lot like roaches. Once you get them in your house, no matter what you do, you can't ever get rid of them. You can buy all kinds of shit to kill 'em, but a lot just leave and come back. We probably gonna do the same thing. The roaches stay or come back 'cause there's a reason: food. We stay or come back cause there's money.

Albert, another older hustler, had this comment:

Listen, we just have to be patient. We been through shit like this before. We gotta ride this out like a lotta other things they throw at us. The worse thing that could happen is we gotta find a new place, so what? The only way it's really gonna hurt us is if they get people to stop buyin' it, and do you think that's gonna happen? Nope! So ain't nothin' really gonna change that much—as long as we chill [stay cool] and ride it out.

The boys' reaction to law enforcement efforts are similarly varied. While some think the increased police presence at the terminal and around the 42nd Street area threaten to eliminate hustling, others have recognized that police resources are limited and cannot control or contain hustling in all parts of the district. Consequently, they simply move away from the pressure and into a less hostile atmosphere a few blocks away.

Scarface: It's like this. They did this survey of people who use the Port Authority and they said it's dirty, they don't like people sleepin' by the gates and stuff, and they don't like hustlers and tricks hangin' around the place. So they started with Operation Alternative, and then they started with lots of undercover cops tryin' to pick up hustlers. Then they started puttin' cops all over the place. They got 'em standin' on every corner outside the Port, they got 'em standin' just inside the front doors, they go up by the gates, and they, like, watch the men's rooms for us. And every time they see us hangin' out anywhere, they tell us to leave.

Yeah, they got lots of cops around here now. But we get by most of them. We know which bathrooms they check out, like the ones far away from everything else. They think we go there because nobody's around. Well we don't go there anymore, because we know that's where they are. And we know most of the DTs around here, so we stay away from them. But, like, the new ones that come in or the undercover guys? We got them too. You know where the glass doors are by the police station is? Well, just down the hall a little bit there's another glass door that ain't marked. We know that's where the undercovers and the detectives hang out, so all we do is stand by the doors and watch who goes in and who goes out. Then we know who they are and we can tell everybody so they don't get caught. It don't work all the time, but it helps. And the thing is, we know what they're about. We know that we can't make the uniforms look bad. They got a job to do, and if he don't do it, then he gonna come down on us. So we try to be chill about it and don't cause no trouble and they leave us alone most of the time. So basically, when they come down on us, we move until the heat's off and then we come back.

Doubletake: Hey, the cops can't be everywhere. You can always tell when they doin' somethin' new, like the undercover cops. All of a sudden we'll see a lot of younger guys lookin' to pick up hustlers. But a lot about bein' good at hustling is to know when and where the cops are hangin' out. And we know whatever they do ain't gonna last forever, so we just move to another part of the Port or go across the street or whatever.

CRIME DISPLACEMENT

One of the criticisms of the redevelopment plans and the law enforcement efforts is that they may do little to reduce crime in the targeted areas. For example, many residents of nearby Clinton, a section of the city just beyond Times Square, fear that cleaning up Times Square will cause the drug dealing, prostitution, and other vice-related activities to move north into their neighborhoods. These criticisms point to a displacement effect of crime.

While crime prevention can take many forms, the most common programs are designed to reduce the number of opportunities offenders have to commit crimes and to make it more difficult for them should they choose to try. These "target-hardening" measures include increased police patrols, improved locks and lighting, and physically marking property so it is more easily identified. While the success of these strategies has been mixed (see Rosenbaum 1987), one question that has been raised is whether the success in one neighborhood comes at the expense of another.

Like prevention, displacement can take many forms: offenders may relocate the site of their activities, select different targets within the original site, alter the timing of violations, or engage in different forms of crime, such as switching from burglary to robbery (Hakim and Rengert 1981). Displacement occurs when an offender attempts to avoid the increased likelihood of apprehension caused by a crime prevention strategy. The offender is pushed out of the community and attracted to a neighborhood which does not have a prevention program.

Related to displacement is the concept of crime spillover. Crime spillover refers simply to the commission of crimes across jurisdictional lines. Spillovers result from a "pull" factor or attraction to a community for some reason (such as increased wealth in that area), whereas crime is displaced when offenders are "pushed" into another area because of preventive efforts (Hakim and Rengart 1981).

RESEARCH ON DISPLACEMENT

The evidence concerning a displacement effect in crime prevention has been mixed (McNamara 1994). In the 1970s, two studies sponsored by the Rand Institute in New York City indicated the presence of the phenomenon. In one, a 40% increase in police manpower in one precinct of New York reduced street crimes there; however, increased numbers of crimes were reported in adjacent precincts (Press 1971).

Additionally, in an effort to reduce the number of robberies on buses in New York City, an exact-fare strategy was implemented. While the number of robberies declined on the buses, the number on the City's subways increased (Chaiken, Lawless and Stevenson 1974). Moreover, Lateef (1974) found that a police helicopter program displaced robberies, burglaries and auto thefts to precincts that lacked such an effort. Similarly, Gabor (1981) found that the Operation Identification program led to a displacement of burglaries in Ottawa to those homes that did not participate. On the other hand, Matthews (1990) found that an increased police effort had no effect on prostitution. Similarly, Repetto (1976), in a study of burglaries pointed out that while it is possible that some crimes may be displaced, most offenders are opportunistic, and thus, situational prevention or target hardening does, in fact, reduce the amount of crime committed in a geographical area.

There are also a number of studies of community-based prevention programs that have found evidence against the displacement effect (see for instance Allatt 1984; Forrester, Chatterton and Pease 1988; Lindsay and McGillis 1986; Schneider 1986). The evidence, then, shows that in some cases, reducing opportunities to commit crimes leads to a decrease in the crime rate, while in others, the activity is simply shifted to a different location. However, displacement is a complicated phenomenon that is influenced by a multitude of factors.

FACTORS CENTRAL TO DISPLACEMENT

Most displacement research focuses on three main factors: the success of the prevention program, the adaptability of offenders, and the offender's motivation. First, the prevention program must be successful in reducing crime in the targeted area. In this way, a program elicits the neccesary response from offenders to cause displacement to take place. In short, offenders must be deterred from certain targets, crimes and areas (Cornish and Clarke 1986).

Second, much of the early crime prevention research acted on the assumption that the offender population is specialized and territorial. However, there is a large body of research indicating that offenders are very adaptable to changing conditions. Offender mobility studies, such as that by Repetto (1976), have pointed out that location is a relatively minor obstacle in the commission of crime.

While there are factors that influence offender mobility (e.g. age of the offender and type of crime), offenders are often willing and able to travel considerable distances to commit crimes—distances probably exceeding the boundaries of a particular prevention program (see also Gabor 1990). Moreover, one of the things that makes displacement so elusive is the versatility of offenders. Preventing burglaries, for example, may simply cause offenders to shift to a different type of offense (Miethe 1991).

Finally, there is evidence that displacement is more likely to occur for less serious property offenses than violent crimes. The basis for this has been the idea that violent crimes tend to be characterized by emotional involvement by the offenders and that attempts to reduce these opportunities are likely to fail since the offenders are unaffected by the potential consequences or the certainty of apprehension (Trasler 1986; Katz 1989).

Another instance of offender motivation that will lead to displacement is drug addiction. Desperate to sustain their habit, addicts will generally ignore most of the risks involved in committing a crime. Other hard-core offenders who have a vested interest in committing certain types of crime are also less likely to be dissuaded (Gabor 1990). This is a critical component in the argument for displacement as the debate below indicates.

SITUATIONAL PREVENTION VERSUS DISPLACEMENT

The basis of the situational approach to prevention is the concept of opportunity (Gabor 1990). Situational measures have been classified into several categories: target hardening, target removal, reduction of profits derived from crime, and increased surveillance (Hough, Clarke and Mayhew 1980). Proponents argue that the presence of an opportunity structure plays a central role in explanations of, and respones to, crime. Most offenders are said to be opportunistic, taking advantage of situations as they emerge. There is a large body of evidence to indicate that if opportunities to commit crimes are apparent, even "ordinary" people can be expected to commit the act (see for example Zimbardo 1973; Gabor 1990; Wallerstein and Wyle 1947; Wilson and Kelling 1982). Thus, the argument is that a great deal of crime is committed by people who merely respond to situational cues and who would not turn to other crimes or targets in the absence of those cues. Since this type of offender comprises the bulk of the criminal population, reducing the number of opportunities can result in a dramatic decrease in overall crime.

In contrast, displacement theorists contend that situational measures do little to prevent violent crimes or highly motivated offenders. Trasler (1986) suggested that murderers and rapists do not tend to respond to an increase in risk-related measures, such as longer sentences. In fact, Gabor (1987) found that only a small proportion of offenders were even aware of newly implemented precautionary measures in a community.

Proponents argue that prevention can, paradoxically, escalate the level and seriousness of crime in an area. For example, armed robbers may end up committing more holdups if situational measures, such as store policies limiting the amount of cash on hand, reduce the amount of profit per incident. In this sense, the amount of displaced crime may actually exceed the amount prevented. With regard to seriousness, the hardening of "finesse" targets such as banks may lead to more crude forms of crime such as mugging citizens (Camp 1967; Haran and Martin 1977; Challinger 1989; Gabor 1987).

The debate continues and no attempt will be made to resolve it here. What is important to consider is that displacement can be a viable and likely reaction by offenders to pressures in a given geographical area, especially by those committing nonviolent offenses. Moreover, these pressures may lead the offender to engage in a variety of responses a few of which include relocation and/or selecting a different target or switching types of crimes.

THE BOYS AND DISPLACEMENT

There is little doubt that the redevelopment of Times Square, law enforcement efforts, and even the civic efforts in Bryant Park have affected the boys. It also appears that the factors that were said to increase the likelihood of a displacement effect also seem to be present in the hustling population. The research on displacement indicates that those offenders who are highly motivated or persistent in committing crimes are less likely to be influenced by target-hardening measures. In the hustling community, this comprises two primary groups: older hustlers and those addicted to crack.

By definition, older hustlers have a higher social standing in the community than younger ones. Many are core members of the group, and they have a vested interest in maintaining the existing structure. They are also the most likely to feel they are an important part of the culture. In short, they have ties to the community and feel they play a central part in it. Additionally, there is an added economic benefit since these hustlers, who are not crackheads, have become more attractive to clients because so many of the young hustlers are. For these reasons, older hustlers like Flacco are simply shifting the location of their activities to the 8th Avenue district. For this group, a displacement effect seems readily apparent.

It also seems that displacement is operating among the younger hustlers, although for slightly different reasons. The research on displacement cites those addicted to drugs as being less likely to be influenced by target-hardening measures. In short, they comprise part of that "highly motivated offender" category. This is especially true of crackheads, who tend to be younger hustlers. They are not intimidated by the prevention strategies, and they, too, have shifted their activities to 8th Avenue.

For nonaddicted, young hustlers, however, it seems that redevelopment is causing not only a shift in location, but also possibly a change in their targets and types of crime. Recall that one potential consequence of target-hardening has been the escalation to more violent offenses. That is, situational prevention in one area can lead to an escalation in the seriousness of crime in another. As the renovation and law enforcement efforts in Times Square reduce opportunities to hustle and changes the location of the existing market, Paco and other hustlers have said they may feel compelled to resort to mugging theatergoers or to engage in other forms of violent street crime as an alternative.

CONCLUSION

Thus, it seems fair to state that the hustling market, as well as the hustling community, are responsive to civic, developmental, and law enforcement efforts to eliminate hustling. With regard to the law enforcement community's efforts, there are essentially two types of crackdowns taking place. One type is designed to remove the market from the area. These types of crackdowns can be referred to as "locale crackdowns," where there is an effort to remove hustling as an activity from a certain location. Examples include efforts in Bryant Park and the Port Authority Bus Terminal.

The other type, which can be referred to as "arrest crackdowns," are those in which there is an effort to target the participants in the activity. In this instance, the targets are clients and hustlers. The undercover operations taking place in and around Times Square, as well as the law enforcement effort carried out prior to the Democratic National Convention, are examples. While each type of effort has somewhat different consequences, the effectiveness of each is predicated on periodic reenforcement. Without it, the market and the participants will simply return to the same place after the sweep has been concluded.

What we are beginning to see, however, is a type of consistent crackdown in the area, which is causing the market and the hustlers to gradually shift toward 8th Avenue. In other words, most of the hustling either has been, or is in the process of being, displaced in one form or another to the 8th Avenue area. Moreover, while these efforts will almost certainly eliminate some types of crime, and may even lead some hustlers to curtail their activities, for the vast majority, there is too much at stake to stop.

With families to feed, drug habits to support, and statuses and identities to preserve, the boys of Times Square will continue to hustle regardless of how much money the City spends on "cleaning up the streets." Additionally, one of the most salient features of the hustling market is the structural characteristics of the area, something law enforcement efforts have been hard-pressed to eliminate. And while the large-scale renovation of Times Square could threaten the market, economic constraints have drastically reduced that plan and allowed the market to simply move a short distance from its original locale.

REFERENCES

Allatt, Patricia. 1984. "Residential Security: Containment and Displacement of Burglary." *Howard Journal* 23:99-116.

Camp, George. 1967. *Nothing to Lose: A Study of Bank Robbery In America*. Michigan: University Microfilms.

Chaiken, Jan M., M. W. Lawless, and K. A. Stevenson. 1974. *The Impact of Police Activity on Crime: Robberies on the New York City Subway System*. New York: New York City Rand Institute.

Challinger, Dennis. 1989. *Armed Robbery: Proceedings of a Seminar*. Canberra: Australian Institute of Criminology.

Cornish, Derek B. and Ronald V. Clarke. 1986. "Understanding Crime Displacement: An Application of Rational Choice Theory." *Criminology* 25:933-943.

Daly, William. Office of Midtown Enforcement. 1993. Telephone interview by author, March 29.

Dunlap, David W. 1992. "Times Square Plan Is on Hold, but Meter Is Still Running." *New York Times* August 9, p. 21.

Forrester, David, Michael Chatterton, and Ken Pease. 1988. *The Kirkholt Burglary Prevention Project, Rochdale*. Home Office Crime Prevention Unit paper 13. London: Home Office.

Gabor, Thomas. 1981. "The Crime Displacement Hypothesis: An Empirical Examination." *Crime and Delinquency* 26:390-404.

Gabor, Thomas. 1987. "Crime by the Public. In Curt Griffiths and Margaret Jacksons eds., *Introduction to Canadian Criminology*. Toronto, Canada: Harcourt Brace Jovanovich.

Gabor, Thomas. 1990. "Crime Displacement and Situational Prevention: Toward the Development of Some Principles." *Canadian Journal of Criminology* 32(1):41-73.

Hakim, Simon, and George Rengert. 1981. *Crime Spillover*. Beverly Hills, Calif.: Sage Publications.

Haran, J. F. and J. M. Martin. 1977. "The Imprisonment of Bank Robbers: The Issue of Deterrence." *Federal Probation* 41:250-56.

Hough, Michael J., Ronald V. Clarke, and Patricia Mayhew. 1980. "Introduction." In Ronald V. Clarke and Patricia Mayhew eds., *Designing Out Crime*. London: Her Majesty's Stationary Office.

Katz, Jack. 1989. *Seductions of Crime*. New York: Basic Books.

Lateef, Barry A. 1974. "Helicopter Patrol in Law Enforcement: An Evaluation." *Journal of Police Science and Administration* 2:62-65.

Lindsay, Betsy, and Daniel McGillis. 1986. "Citywide Community Crime Prevention: An Assessment of the Seattle Program." In Dennis Rosenbaum ed. *Community Crime Prevention*. 46-67. Beverly Hills, Calif.: Sage Publications.

Matthews, Roger. 1990. "Developing More Effective Strategies for Curbing Prostitution." *Security Journal* 3(3):182-187.

McNamara, Robert P. ed. 1994. *Crime Displacement: The Other Side of Prevention*. New York: Cummings and Hathaway.

Miethe, Terrance 1991. "Citizen-Based Crime Control Activity and Victimization Risks: An Examination of Displacement and Free-Rider Effects." *Criminology* 29(3):419-439.

Newmark, Shane. 1991. "Times Square: a Changing Story" Unpublished report for the New York State Urban Development Corporation.

New York City Police Department. Office of Midtown Enforcement. 1989 Crime Report.

New York City Police Department. 1991 Crime Report.

New York City Police Department. 1992 Crime Report.

New York Port Authority Bus Terminal Police. 1992. Crime Report.

New York Port Authority Bus Terminal Police. 1993. Crime Report.

New York State Urban Development Corporation. 42nd Street Development Project. 1992. "Crossroads: A Changing Times Square." July.

New York State Urban Development Corporation. 42nd Street Development Project. 1989. "42nd Street Project Receives a Wide Range of Entertainment Proposals for Six Theaters." Press Release, May 10.

Press, James S. 1971. *Some Effect of an Increase in Police Manpower in the 20th Precinct in New York City*. New York: Rand Institute.

Repetto, Thomas. 1976. "Crime Prevention and the Displacement Phenomenon." *Crime and Delinquency* 22:166-177.

Rosenbaum, Dennis. 1987. "The Theory and Research Behind Neighborhood Watch: Is it a Sound Fear and Crime Reduction Strategy?" *Crime and Delinquency* 33:103-134.

Schneider, Anne. 1986. "Neighborhood-based Antiburglary Strategies: An Analysis of Public and Private Benefits from the Portland Program." In Dennis Rosenbaum ed. *Community Crime Prevention, Does it Work?* 68-86. Beverly Hills, Calif: Sage Publications.

Trasler, Gordon. 1986. "Situational Crime Control and Rational Choice: A Critique." In Kevin Heal and Gloria Laycock eds. *Situational Crime Prevention*. London: Her Majesty's Stationary Office.

Wallerstein, James, and Charles J. Wyle. 1947. "Our Law-abiding Lawbreakers." *Probation* 25:107-112.

Wilson, James Q., and George Kelling. 1982. "Broken Windows." *Atlantic Monthly* pp. 31-39.

Zimbardo, Phillip. 1973. "A Field Experiment in Auto Shaping." In Colin Ward ed. *Vandalism*. London: Architectural Press.

8

Epilogue

In December, after my time with the boys had ended, I continued to maintain contact with a few hustlers by telephone. In a few instances we exchanged telephone numbers, but the most common arrangement was that I gave them my home number and told them to call collect. In this way I was able to maintain close ties with Flacco, Canno, and Apache, who provided me with updates on different hustlers as well as what was going on in their own lives.

From January to May 1993, I made periodic trips to Times Square, either to collect information or to simply see what changes had taken place and how the boys were doing. I also used these opportunities to give the boys versions of chapters to comment on and evaluate. I promised them early on in the project that if they were interested in the finished product, I would allow them to critique my work. Only Apache and Flacco were interested but the feedback I received from them was very positive. They stated that the facts and circumstances of events were correct: I had accurately told their story.

Eddie has found a sugar daddy. He has given up his apartment and lives with this man, but has not told him of his HIV status, and does not intend to. For now, Eddie is supplied with money and clothing and spends most of his time in the bars socializing. He rarely ventures out during the day. He has begun to experiment with crack as well. Eddie has had sugar dadies in the past and, in all likelihood, the arrangement will soon come to an end and he will return to the Times Square scene.

Canno continues to preach his knowledge to young hustlers and continues his volunteer efforts, especially with AIDS patients. His recovery from his injuries is nearly complete, and the last time I saw him, he was returning from an interview for a job as a waiter. He did not get the job, but he was not discouraged, and says he will try again.

"When you get this close to dyin', not gettin' a job ain't no big thing," he says.

Mad Max has succumbed to the temptations of crack. He is thoroughly addicted and has fallen into the trap of many crackhead hustlers. Perhaps the smartest of the group in terms of abstract intelligence, he has become yet another victim to the drug. Max is now often found huddled in a corner or doorway. He has an additional problem in that he has stolen drugs from the Colombian dealer for whom he worked. The dealer swore revenge, so Max spends most of his time "looking over his shoulder."

Flacco continues to hang around the Port Authority and the peep shows. He hustles perhaps once or twice a week which, he says, is by choice. He says he has kept a journal of all his hustling activities and experiences and wants to write a book about his life. He can usually be found roaming the streets of Times Square, waving to some, knowing most, and generally accepting the status that his experience in the trade has accorded him.

Like Flacco, his long-time friend, Apache continues to remain in the Times Square area. His son is now eighteen months old, and Apache says he spends his days chasing him around the apartment. He continues to go to Streetworks Project for groceries and counseling and recently received notification that his Social Security benefits had been approved. Apache still hustles for spending money and to provide for his family, but unfortunately, he has also begun to experience a number of medical problems. He was recently treated for thrush, an infection of the throat common in HIV/AIDS patients, and has also developed a kidney infection. While he has not yet been hospitalized, he is beginning to realize that the virus presents serious problems for him. He turned twenty-two in February.

Pretty Boy Tony works for a home health care organization. He is a nurse's aide who spends his nights taking care of an elderly man who has cancer. He says he has a lot of free time since he works the late shift when the man is often asleep. It's an easy job and it keeps him off the street at night. His shift ends at 8 a.m., and then he comes home to his aunt's house. He is not getting along with her, but since they work opposite shifts, he rarely sees her. He is saving for an apartment and hopes to go to school to study nursing. On weekends, he can still be found on 8th Avenue. Tony has finally decided which "team" to play for: he says he is now a confirmed homosexual.

Uzi, a drug dealer who hustles when he cannot make ends meet, was caught with a large quantity of crack in his possession during the sweep of Times Square (before the Democratic National Convention) and is presently in prison in upstate New York. Panhead was caught trying to rob a local convenience store. Like Uzi, he dabbled in drug dealing when the opportunity arose. In addition to this offense, he was also wanted for an aggravated assault charge. Unable to make bond, he is currently on Riker's Island awaiting trial.

Deadhead could not find the friends who left him in New York City, so he gave up looking and instead tried to contact other friends in the Florida area. When this attempt was not successful, he decided to move to New Orleans. He and a companion each bought a bus ticket, packed what few belongings they had, and left New York in the hopes of finding more lucrative opportunities in the French Quarter. No one has heard from him. Paco, Melvin, Playboy, Scarface, Smokealot, Watchdog, and Jose were arrested during the sweep, and their current status is unknown. What happened to the others is also unknown: few have been seen, and even fewer have been heard from.

These are but a few of the boys I have come to know in Times Square. In my many conversations with them, none had any real idea what their future would hold, or even what they would like it to hold. Even for hustlers like Mad Max or Flacco, who once had dreams of going to college, the vision is so blurred by the day-to-day struggles that any hopes of fulfilling the dream are nearly impossible.

THE IDEA OF COMMUNITY

In chapter 1, I stated that I viewed the hustlers of Times Square as a community. We typically look on communities as possessing certain characteristics or clearly defined features that serve to identify them, but in this instance those features are not always clear, nor are they always formalized. Despite this fact, the community somehow remains intact and functional for the boys.

In one sense, there are fairly clear characteristics. For instance, there is a normative dimension or internal component of the community that sets out a number of relatively clear rules dictating the nature of transactions with clients, the relationships with other hustlers, and the sense of responsibility that members feel for each other. There is also a sense of cohesion and loyalty felt by the members of this community whereby hustlers protect one another from the many threats they face. This loyalty is bred in part from survival needs, but it is also a product of the existing normative structure. In short, the boys have created a social order that allows the nature of their interactions and professional behavior to follow an essentially predictable pattern. However, this normative structure may be changing due to the impact of the influx of crack.

Another dimension of this community involves its dependence on the larger collectivity. The hustling community exists primarily because of its symbiotic relationship with the other groups and organizations that make up the hustling market and the Times Square scene. The boys depend on the peep shows, the bus terminal, local bars, hotels, and similar establishments in order to operate effectively. If these institutions are removed through the proposed redevelopment efforts, the viability of the market could be threatened. However, large-scale redevelopment efforts have been postponed, and stepped-up law enforcement efforts are causing the locale of the market to gradually shift from 42nd Street toward 8th Avenue.

Another important factor in examining this community is how, when, and where the boys meet to interact and spend time together. These types of interactions are very important in developing the sense of cohesion and loyalty they feel toward each other. While the favored hustling locations provide a steady source of customers for the boys, they also serve as a gathering place to meet and socialize. Other locations are used for specific purposes, such as the parks where the boys play handball.

Also included, but playing a more limited role in the community, are the drug dealers, phone card thieves, and the con men who dot the Times Square landscape. These groups, and the role they play in the Times Square scene, were only given marginal attention in this study due to a more concentrated focus on the hustlers themselves. However, they make an important contribution to the structure of the marketplace and to the hustling community. The hustlers, then, are dependent on many others in the area, and vice versa. Without these organizations, relationships, and agreements, it would be difficult, if not impossible, for either the market or the community to survive. The nature of the roles played by the principal actors is another feature of this community. These roles are loose and not clearly defined, but in terms of their significance, or impact, the lack of clarity does not seem to matter. For instance, while many of the boys recognize Apache and Flacco as leaders in the community, these roles are not formally designated nor does a social hierarchy exists for other roles. Nonetheless, virtually every hustler in the Times Square scene knows and understands Apache's and Flacco's places in their world. How and when they acquired their status and position is unknown. All that is known is that the position is important, they occupy it, and as such, they are to be treated with respect. However, just as crack is causing a breakdown of the normative structure of the community, it is also affecting the social position of its leaders. While still subtle in presentation, a few crackheads have begun to disregard the status accorded to the community elders, either by challenging their position as leaders or by attempting to steal steady clients from them.

Another organizational feature involves how news and other information is circulated. There is a rather extensive and accurate information network. When someone is arrested for example, it does not take very long to discover who is involved and what they have done. Similarly, the news of Raul's death circulated quickly, with most of the boys learning of it shortly after it occurred. In the same way, news of police sweeps or new strategies being implemented to combat hustling are passed along to each other. However, speculation, rumors, and misinformation about AIDS are challenging the efficacy of this network.

The boys pass along information to each other concerning effective means of prevention as well as news about infected clients and other hustlers. The vast majority of their preventive efforts are ineffective, and the existent rumors have caused some hustlers to become skeptical about, or even ignore entirely, a great deal of the information that is circulated within the community.

Thus, while there is a strong sense of cohesion and loyalty among the members, there are a number of changes taking place in the area that dramatically affects the community. Moreover, despite the collective and individual responses, it seems that these problems may be larger than the community's ability to accommodate them.

THE FUTURE OF HUSTLING IN TIMES SQUARE

Hustling in Times Square is changing, and although it will continue to exist, the nature and structure of the community has been significantly altered. While it is true there will always be a market for hustlers since there is a demand for the product they sell, in the future this population could easily consist primarily of crackheads and older boys, each group vying for a client population that is finding these types of sexual exchanges to be increasingly risky propositions.

These two groups, while currently at odds, could coexist if they had to, but the sense of community and social cohesion that were once felt would probably be eliminated. Gone will be the days when a certain etiquette regulated the transactions or when one boy willingly sacrificed his own trick to keep an eye on a buddy. Gone, too, will be the one thing that kept many boys going: the opportunity to feel like a part of something greater than themselves. Thus, while the trade will likely continue, what will change is the very thing that once made it be a relatively safe and stable phenomenon.

CONCLUSION

This project began as an attempt to examine how high-risk groups deal with AIDS, and turned into a study of a community and the pressures it faces. While immersing myself in this culture, I learned there were a host of problems for the boys beyond the physical dangers of the trade. They must contend with the influence of crack, deal with the obvious risks of acquiring AIDS, and cope with the pressures of urban progress as the city attempts to restore Times Square.

I also learned that there is a sense of community among the boys of Times Square, but that social changes are causing this community to fragment. Moreover, while hustling will remain a part of Times Square's future, the future of the community of hustlers is uncertain: the boys face a number of formidable obstacles, and it is not clear that the hustler community can overcome them.

Selected Bibliography

Becker, Howard. 1963. *The Outsiders: Studies in the Sociology of Deviance.* New York: The Free Press.

Bloom, Ken. 1991. *Broadway: An Encyclopedic Guide to the History, People and Places of Times Square.* New York: Facts on File.

Borus-Rotheram, Mary, and Cheryl Koopman. 1991. "Sexual Risk Behaviors, AIDS Knowledge and Beliefs about AIDS among Runaways." *American Journal of Public Health* 81(2):206-208.

Bourgois, Phillipe. 1989. "In Search of Horatio Alger: Culture and Ideology in the Crack Economy." *Contemporary Drug Problems* 16(4):619-50.

Bourgois, Phillipe, and Eloise Dunlap. 1993. "Exorcising Sex-for-Crack: An Ethnographic Perspective from Harlem." In Mitchell Ratner ed., *Crack Pipe as Pimp*, 97-132. New York: Lexington Books.

Boyle, Kathleen, and Douglas M. Anglin. 1993. "To the Curb: Sex Bartering and Drug Use Among Homeless Crack Users in Los Angeles." In Mitchell Ratner ed. *Crack Pipe as Pimp*, 159-186. New York: Lexington Books.

Butts, William Marlin. 1947. "Boy Prostitutes of the Metropolis." *Journal of Clinical Psychopathology* 8:673-681.

Calhoun, Thomas, and Brian Pickerill. 1988. "Young Male Prostitutes: Their Knowledge of Selected Sexually Transmitted Diseases." *Psychology: A Journal of Human Behavior* 25(3/4):1-8.

Campagna, Daniel J., and Donald L. Poffenberger. 1988. *The Sexual Trafficking of Children.* South Hadley, Mass.: Auburn House.

Caukins, Sivan E., and Neil R. Coombs. 1976. "The Psychodynamics of Male Prostitution." *American Journal of Psychotherapy* 30:441-451.

Coombs, Neil. 1974. "Male Prostitution: A Psychological View of Behavior." *American Journal of Orthopsychiatry* 44(5):782-789.

Cornish, Derek B., and Ronald V. Clarke. 1986. "Understanding Crime Displacement: An Application of Rational Choice Theory." *Criminology* 25:933-943.

Drew, Dennis, and Jonathan Drake. 1969. *Boys For Sale*. New York: Brown Book Company.

Elifson, Kurt, Jacqueline Boles, and Michael Sweat. 1993. "Risk Factors Associated with HIV Infection Among Male Prostitutes." *American Journal of Public Health* 83:79-83.

Erenberg, Lewis A. 1981. *Steppin' Out*. Westport, Conn.: Greenwood Press.

Fagan, Jeffery, and Ko-lin Chin. 1989. "Initiation into Crack and Cocaine." *Contemporary Drug Problems* 16(4):579-618.

Flynn, John C. 1991. *Cocaine*. New York: Birch Lane Press.

Gabor, Thomas. 1990. "Crime Displacement and Situational Prevention: Toward the Development of Some Principles." *Canadian Journal of Criminology* 32(1):41-73.

Goffman, Erving. 1959. *The Presentation of Self in Everyday Life*. New York: Doubleday.

Goode, Eric. 1989. *Drugs in American Society*. 3rd ed. New York: McGraw-Hill.

Grinspoon, Lester, and James B. Bakalar. 1985. *Cocaine: A Drug and Its Social Evolution*. New York: Basic Books.

Hakim, Simon, and George Rengert. 1981. *Crime Spillover*. Beverly Hills, Calif.: Sage Publications.

Humphreys, Laud. 1970. *Tearoom Trade: Impersonal Sex in Public Places*. London: Duckworth.

Inciardi, James. 1992. *The War on Drugs II*. Mountain View, Calif.: Mayfield Publishing Company.

Inciardi, James, Dorothy Lockwood, and Anne E. Pottieger 1993a. *Street Kids, Street Drugs, Street Crime*. Belmont, Calif.: Wadsworth Publishing.

Inciardi, James, Dorothy Lockwood, and Anne E. Pottieger. 1993b. *Women and Crack-Cocaine*. New York: Macmillan.

James, Jennifer. 1982. *Entrance into Male Prostitution*. Washington, D.C.: National Institute of Mental Health.

Jersild, Jens. 1956. *Boy Prostitution*. Copenhagen, Denmark: C. E. Gad.

Kaslow, Richard A., and Donald Francis. 1989. *The Epidemiology of AIDS: Expression, Occurrence and Control of Human Immunodeficiency Virus Type 1 Infection*. New York: Oxford University Press.

Katz, Jack. 1989. *Seductions of Crime*. New York: Basic Books.

Kornblum, William, and Terry Williams. 1994. *West Forty-Second Street: The Bright Light Zone*. New York: Basic Books (forthcoming).

Lauderback, David, and Donald Waldorf. 1989. "Male Prostitution and AIDS: Preliminary Findings." *Focus: A Guide to AIDS Research* Jan. 3-4.

Lee, David. 1981. *Cocaine Handbook: An Essential Reference*. San Rafael, Calif.: What if? Publishing.

Luckenbill, David. 1985. "Dynamics of the Deviant Sale." *Deviant Behavior* 5(1):131-151.

Luckenbill, David. 1986a. "Deviant Career Mobility: The Case of Male Prostitution." *Social Problems* 33(4):283-296.

Luckenbill, David. 1986b. "Entering Male Prostitution." *Urban Life* 14(2):131-153.

MacDonald, Pat; Dan Waldorf; Craig Reinarmen; and Sheigla Murphy. 1988. "Heavy Cocaine Use and Sexual Behavior." *Journal of Drug Issues* 18:437-455.

MacNamara, Donal E. J. 1965. "Male Prostitution in American Cities: A Socioeconomic or Pathological Phenomenon?" *American Journal of Orthopsychiatry* 35:204.

McKeganey, Neil, Marina Barnard, and Michael Bloor. 1990. "A Comparison of HIV-related Risk Behavior and Risk Reduction Between Female Street Working Prostitutes and Male Rent Boys in Glasgow." *Sociology of Health and Illness* 12(3):274-292.

McNamara, Robert P. 1991. "From Prophylactics to Prayers: The Reactions to AIDS by Juvenile Male Prostitutes." Paper presented at the Eastern Sociological Society, Providence, RI. April.

McNamara, Robert P. ed. 1994. *Crime Displacement: The Other Side of Prevention.* New York: Cummings and Hathaway.

Miller, Walter. 1958. "Lower-Class Culture as a Generating Milieu of Gang Delinquency." *Journal of Social Issues* 14:5-19.

New York City Police Department. 1992. Office of Midtown Enforcement, City of New York. *Summary of Criminal Activity on West 42nd Street: Eighth Avenue to Seventh Avenue, 1980-91.*

Perloff, Linda. 1983. "Perceptions of Vulnerability to Victimization." *Journal of Social Issues* 39(2):41-61.

Pleak, Richard R., and Heino Meyer-Bahlburg. 1990. "Sexual Behavior and AIDS Knowledge of Young Male Prostitutes in Manhattan." *Journal of Sex Research* 27(4):557-587.

Ratner, Mitchell ed. 1993. *Crack Pipe as Pimp.* New York: Lexington Books.

Reiss, Albert J., Jr. 1961. "The Social Integration of Queers and Peers." *Social Problems* 9(2):102-20.

Repetto, Thomas. 1976. "Crime Prevention and the Displacement Phenomenon." *Crime and Delinquency* 22:166-77.

Rosenbaum, Dennis. 1987. "The Theory and Research behind Neighborhood Watch: Is It a Sound Fear and Crime Reduction Strategy?" *Crime and Delinquency* 33:103-34.

Ross, Laurence H. 1959. "The Hustler in Chicago." *Journal of Student Research* 1:13-19.

Sellin, Thorsten. 1938. "Culture Conflict and Crime." Social Science Research Council. *Bulletin No. 41.* New York: Social Science Research Council, pp. 63-70.

Trasler, Gordon. 1986. "Situtational Crime Control and Rational Choice: A Critique." In Kevin Heal and Gloria Laycock eds. *Situational Crime Prevention*. London: Her Majesty's Stationary Office.

Waldorf, Dan. 1976. *Careers in Dope*. Clifton Hills, N.J.: Prentice-Hall.

Waldorf, Dan; Sheigla Murphy; David Lauderback; Craig Reinarman; and Toby Marotta. 1990. "Needle Sharing Among Male Prostitutes: Preliminary Findings of the Prospero Project." *The Journal of Drug Issues* 20(2):309-334.

Weinstein, Neil D. 1984. "Why It Won't Happen to Me: Perceptions of Risk Factors and Susceptibility." *Health Psychology* 3:431-457.

Weisberg, Kelly D. 1985. *Children of the Night*. South Hadley, Mass.: Lexington Books.

Williams, Terry M. 1992. *The Crackhouse: Notes From the End of the Line*. Reading, Mass: Addison-Wesley.

Index

About the Author

ROBERT P. MCNAMARA is Assistant Professor of Sociology at Furman University. He is the author of *Crime Displacement: The Other Side of Prevention* (1994), *Sex, Scams and Street Life: The Sociology of New York City's Times Square* (Praeger, forthcoming), *Sex, Drugs and HIV* (forthcoming) with Cindy Patton, and *The Urban Landscape: Selected Readings* (forthcoming) with Kristy McNamara. He has been a consultant for state, federal, and private agencies on topics such as AIDS, drug abuse, and policing.